The Son of Love
and the Birth of the New Mysteries

RON MACFARLANE

Published 2014 by
Greater Mysteries Publications
Mission, BC, Canada

Cover Design: Ron MacFarlane

Printed in the United States of America

ISBN:
ISBN-13: 978-0994007711
ISBN-10: 099400771X

DEDICATION

Special thanks to my dear wife, Anne Marie, for her unwavering and enthusiastic support and understanding as I faithfully followed my literary dreams in our precious retirement years.

CONTENTS

The Son of Love

INTRODUCTION

* Background into the Ancient Mysteries

SINCE THE PREHISTORIC dawn of mankind, there have always been two classes of people: leaders and followers. Leaders have always been few, and followers have always been many.

Prior to the last Great Flood, leadership was instilled in the few by beings more advanced than nascent humanity—superphysical angel beings—for reasons similar to the role of parents and children today; that is, for guidance, education and protection.

While our ancient ancestors did possess a dim, pictorial awareness of the supernatural world around them, their waking consciousness was indistinct and dreamlike without a strong sense of separate individuality. Not surprisingly, then, they were easily influenced and directed by these more advanced beings.

Throughout the ages, in various parts of the earth, small groups of suitably chosen individuals were directed to establish sacred centres of higher learning where they would be trained and educated by their invisible spirit guides to provide leadership. It was from these sanctuary centres that wise direction was given to the great mass of primitive mankind. These were the ancient wellsprings of civilizing knowledge such as the use of fire, the smelting of metals, the practices of healing, the domestication of animals and the development of cultural arts: language, architecture, painting, sculpture, music and drama.

Very early on in human development, then, wisdom and understanding were carefully sieved into two distinct gradations: a finer, more comprehensive knowledge guardedly accessible to the few who had been properly trained in the supernaturally-guided sanctuaries; and a simpler, more basic knowledge of the world conveyed to the general mass of humanity by representatives of the wisdom centres who acted as their leaders.

For vast stretches of human prehistory, this social division of esoteric, inner wisdom restricted to a few inspired leaders, together with an exoteric, outer knowledge disseminated to the vast followers of ordinary humanity, worked as a progressive arrangement in human development. But over time, as mankind gradually evolved dim powers of intellectual reasoning and increased self-awareness, the ancient dreamy perception of superphysical reality steadily disappeared. This naturally resulted in decreased contact with and awareness of the supernatural teachers of mankind in the wisdom sanctuaries.

By the time of the rise of ancient Greek civilization, roughly 2600 years ago, the wisdom sanctuaries had devolved into jealously-guarded repositories of supernatural knowledge retained in the form of symbolic pictures, mythic stories, ritual ceremonies and dramatic presentations. Any direct contact with the superphysical realms of existence had then to be artificially induced with a dangerous, death-like trance condition for three days.

The esoteric sanctuaries at that time were known as Mystery schools, Mystery religions, or simply as, "the

Mysteries" (from the Greek word, "mystērion," meaning 'secret rites'). Those who had first-hand experience of the superphysical through the "temple trance" procedure were known as "initiates". Though these centres were in decline during the time of Greek civilization, their knowledge was still sublime, their ceremonies were still impressive and their cultural and political influence was still considerable—throughout Europe, Asia and the Middle East. Some examples of these diverse Mystery centres known to ordinary history are the Hibernian Mysteries in Ireland, the Druidic Mysteries in Britain, the Eleusinian Mysteries in Greece, the Isis Mysteries in Egypt and the Mithras Mysteries in Persia.

All these Mystery centres continued to maintain the age-old division of advanced knowledge of the supernatural (in Greek, "gnosis") accessible only to initiates—termed the "greater mysteries" and the more elementary knowledge available to the general public—termed the "lesser mysteries."

With the rise of ancient Roman culture, the Mysteries became increasingly corrupted and decadent, slowly dying out as influential and recognized social institutions. As well, initiates even lost the ability to consciously experience the supernatural through trance techniques. Nevertheless, there continued to be a few isolated individuals and communities that retained some dim, atavistic clairvoyant ability even up to the early Renaissance period; and some shadowy remnants of the greater mysteries have survived, even to the present day, within secretive brotherhoods such as Freemasonry.

*   The Incarnation of the Son of Love

Any conscious connection with supernatural reality would have disappeared entirely from human experience, and mankind would have steadily succumbed to the physical forces of destruction and dissolution if the most momentous event in human history had not occurred—the birth of the "Light of the World," the incarnation of the Son of Love—Christ-Jesus.

This powerful event arrested human decline, and the Risen Saviour's victory over sin, sickness, evil and death has once again opened the gates of heaven; that is, provided mankind with the opportunity to access superphysical reality and existence once again.

The story of his life, death, resurrection and ascension is recorded in some detail in the various writings of the New Testament. This information has been faithfully guarded and promoted by the universal institution he established—his Body the Church.

What many in our day are not aware of (or do not accept) is that the founder of Christianity, Christ-Jesus himself, established a two-fold division in his Church, similar but not identical to the ancient Mysteries: an outer, exoteric stream of Christianity which teaches the lesser mysteries of his life; and an inner, esoteric stream of Christianity which teaches the greater mysteries of his life. Within the exoteric body of Christ is found the more basic and abbreviated knowledge (yet sacred and profound) that is accessible to the simple and the educated alike, together with a developmental path leading to Christ-Jesus in the superphysical realm—the path of Mystic-Christianity. Within the esoteric body of Christ is found a deeper, more penetrating knowledge once accessible only to the initiated apostles, but now increasingly accessible to all who seek it, together with a different developmental path leading to Christ-Jesus in the superphysical realm—the path of Rosicrucian-Christianity.

The founder of Christianity has established exoteric and esoteric Christianity as complementary divisions of his Body the Church. Exoteric Christianity was instituted and promoted through St. Peter, and esoteric Christianity was instituted and promoted through St. John.[1] The stream of exoteric Christianity was destined by Christ-Jesus to be a universal religion (and theology) that would remain constant and enduring throughout the centuries. The stream of esoteric Christianity, on the other hand, was destined by Christ-Jesus to be a universal philosophy (and theosophy)—not a religion—that would alter its approach to suit the changing times. Both streams are divinely intended to provide mutually compatible avenues to the truth. Unfortunately, over the past two thousand years these two streams have often been turbulently hostile and inimical to each other, thereby arresting true Christian progress and development. Even to this day, sectarian adherents of each stream fervently maintain that their approach is the only true one, and the other approach is a false path to the Saviour. Christianity in the future will only develop in a positive way through the unifying interpenetration of these two sacred wisdom streams.

Before examining the new mysteries established by Christ-Jesus, it will be necessary to distinguish them from the older, pre-Christian mysteries. The new Christian mysteries are not simply an extension, continuance or altered form of the mysteries that existed before. Analogously, mainstream Christianity is not simply an extension, continuation or alteration of the Judaism that existed before, but something entirely new and different. The depleted pagan mysteries had run their course and were no longer useful or effective, thereby necessitating the birth of the new Christian mysteries in order to establish a bright new avenue of entry into the supernatural realm of existence for all mankind.

Moreover, the new mysteries of Christ-Jesus have efficacious power since this knowledge is born out of the highest truth. This new wisdom, then, is spiritually transformative and far exceeds the "gnosis" (secret knowledge) of the old Mysteries. By embracing these new

Christian mysteries, we "put away our old self and develop the new." As St. Paul eloquently stated centuries before: "[A]s the truth is in [Christ] Jesus. Put off your old nature which belongs to your former manner of life … and be renewed in the spirit of your minds, and put on the new nature, created after the likeness of God in true righteousness and holiness" (Eph 4: 22–24).

*   The Luciferic Intrusion into Anthroposophy

Modern-day esoteric study demands clear intellection and the stringent, testable determination of supersensible facts. Unfortunately, within the esoteric movement of anthroposophy a number of erroneous concepts have taken root that are slowly undermining the true mission and purpose as established by Rudolf Steiner. Steiner repeatedly emphasized that anthroposophy was intended as a historically-new, completely contemporary method of acquiring supersensible knowledge—an authentic "science of the spirit." The primary focus of spiritual science is, of course, to intellectually comprehend the new mysteries of the Son as established by Christ-Jesus.

Even before Steiner's death in 1925, however, an incipient notion began to spread among certain students of Rudolf Steiner that regarded anthroposophy as a continuation of the ancient pagan Mysteries. Rather than seeing the Christmas Conference in 1923–24 as the public inauguration of the General Anthroposophical Society, certain attendees erroneously regarded the event as the "founding of the new Mysteries."[2] Rudolf Steiner was naturally regarded as the initiate-founder of these new Mysteries. Not surprisingly, then, the building established in 1924 as the headquarters for the world-wide General Anthroposophical Society—the Goetheanum—was celebrated by some as a modern-day "temple" for these new Mysteries. Moreover, rather than being "Christ Mysteries" or "Mysteries of the Son," these new Mysteries were often referred to as "Michael Mysteries."

At first, all this misinterpretation seems rather odd considering that Rudolf Steiner was unequivocally clear that the true Christian mysteries were established by Christ-Jesus and that the mission of anthroposophy was to understand these greater mysteries in a spiritually-scientific way. As far back as 27 November 1906 in a lecture entitled, "Esoteric Christianity," Steiner definitively declared:

> At the time of Christ Jesus, to the Mysteries of the Spirit were added the <u>Mysteries of the Son</u>, and these have been ever since the time of Christ. The <u>Mysteries of the Father</u>—the Mysteries of the Future—are only cultivated in a very small circle. The Mysteries of the Son are cultivated in the Rosicrucian Mystery which is also Christian, for those who require a Christianity that is armed to meet all Wisdom … Today we will concern ourselves with the Mysteries of the Son, and see how they differ from the ancient heathen Mysteries. If we would grasp what a mighty step forward has been taken by the coming of Christianity …
>
> An esoteric Christianity does exist … exoteric Christianity is more simple and popular, it speaks to the heart, to the feelings; while esoteric Christianity is essentially deeper than all oriental esoteric. The truth is, the Christian esotericism is the most profound which has ever been brought to mankind. Christian esotericism was <u>brought to the earth</u> by that very Being Himself with whom one must be united.

So what explains this persistent, unanthroposophical mass-delusion, considering that Rudolf Steiner was not the source? What best accounts for this misplaced nostalgic sentiment to connect anthroposophy with the "ancient heathen Mysteries" and to replace the school of spiritual science with a new Mystery school? Part of this question can be explained by the simple misunderstanding of what Rudolf Steiner said and did. For example, establishing a world-wide public society with an "esoteric" centre does not automatically transform the institution into a Mystery school (or religion). Designing and constructing a supersensibly-inspired building (the Goetheanum) for the purpose of performing "mystery plays" does not transform the building into a "Mystery temple" any more than performing a kindergarten Christmas "nativity play" transforms the school into a church. Moreover, studying the ancient pagan Mysteries in a spiritually-scientific way does not connect anthroposophy with these Mysteries any more than studying ancient pagan Mysteries in an empirically-scientific way connects anthropology with these Mysteries. Furthermore, acting under the inspiration and direction of advanced celestial beings does not mean that these actions are by definition "Mystery events."

It is certainly true that specific statements made by Rudolf Steiner about the Christmas Conference could easily be misinterpreted if not considered in the overall context of his prior information. For example, in a lecture given shortly after the Conference on 22 April 1924 entitled, "The Mysteries of Ephesus. The Aristotelian Categories," Steiner stated the following:

> It is indeed the case that when that spiritual impulse which has gone forth from here, from the Goetheanum through the Christmas Foundation meeting, really finds its way into the life of the Anthroposophical Society—(the Society leading on to the [School of Spiritual Science] Classes partially begun)—this Anthroposophical Society will provide the foundation for the Mysteries of the future. The future life of the Mysteries must consciously and deliberately be planted by this Anthroposophical Society.

The "Mysteries of the future" being referred to here are, of course, the Mysteries of the Father (see previous quotation). Providing a "foundation" for them does not mean that Rudolf Steiner intended on "founding new Mysteries," but rather that the Anthroposophical Society should begin to provide a welcoming esoteric environment wherein these future mysteries (to be revealed by the Father) can be studied and understood in a spiritually-scientific way.

Another misinterpreted statement made by Rudolf Steiner in the months following the Christmas Conference was in a lecture given on 12 August 1924:

> Much that remained a Michael secret had therefore to be carried onward in the heart of the Anthroposophical Movement itself—above all the truths relating to historical connections of the kind to which reference has been made. But for a certain time now—actually for months—it has been possible for me to speak of these things without reserve. That is why I have been able to speak freely of the connections between earthly lives, and shall also do so here. For this is part of the unveiling of those Michael Mysteries which took the course I have described to you. (Published in *Cosmic Christianity and the Impulse of Michael*; 1953)

Some anthroposophists have alleged that the "new Mysteries" founded by Rudolf Steiner during the Christmas Conference were "Michael Mysteries." But nowhere in the statutes of the General Anthroposophical Society does Steiner declare that the agenda of the Conference is to found new Michael Mysteries (though he does refer to the Goetheanum as "a school of Spiritual Science"). Besides, what does Steiner mean by "Michael Mysteries"?

Since St. Michael is well-recognized as the great servant of Christ-Jesus, his anthroposophical mission (through Rudolf Steiner) was certainly not to supplant the greater Mysteries of the Son with his own lesser Mysteries. As Steiner himself declared: "Michael is … the Spirit whose task in our epoch is to bring about a deeper, more esoteric understanding of the truths of Christianity" (From a lecture given on 21 August 1924 and published in *Cosmic Christianity and the Impulse of Michael*; 1953). What Steiner means by Michael Mysteries is simply esoteric Christian information revealed by St. Michael concerning karmic biographies and relationships.

Aside from intellectual misinterpretation, what most accounts for the persistent and pervasive misrepresentation of anthroposophy by its very own members is the fact that the society does indeed have an esoteric centre; that is, it is connected to the superphysical realm through its affiliation with the Rosicrucian Order. This of course means that the General Anthroposophical Society is under constant esoteric assault by inimical superphysical beings. Not surprisingly, Lucifer is one such prominent being whose strategy is often to covertly infiltrate persons and organizations and then to subtly direct their attention away from the present to the blissfully nostalgic past.[3] By deceptively directing the focus of anthroposophical members away from the true, present-day Christocentric mission of spiritual science, Lucifer can gradually corrupt the society from within and eventually render it esoterically ineffectual.

Appropriate attention then is drawn away from correctly regarding the Christmas Conference as the "public event" whereby Rudolf Steiner founded the General Anthroposophical Society to, instead, Luciferically regarding the Conference as the "Mystery event" whereby Rudolf Steiner founded the "new Michael Mysteries." Likewise, attention is drawn away from correctly regarding the second Goetheanum as the headquarters of the General Anthroposophical Society and the School of Spiritual Science to, instead, Luciferically regarding the building as the temple of the new Mysteries and the new Michaelic Mystery School.

A further Luciferic characteristic that applies in this case is the impulse to exaggerate, to over-extend, to hyper-inflate or to expand beyond reasonable proportions. By overly-embellishing the true meaning and significance of the Christmas Conference and the Goetheanum, the overall mission of anthroposophical spiritual science is Luciferically distorted and falsified.

Moreover, Rudolf Steiner's statements concerning "Cosmic Christianity" can easily fall prey to recognizably Luciferic distension. The following statement also from the lecture given on 21 August 1924 (published in *Cosmic Christianity and the Impulse of Michael*) serves as a good example:

> [V]ery many who now feel the urge to come to the Anthroposophical Movement ... in the life between death and a new birth ... thronged around Michael, preparing to carry down a Cosmic Christianity again to the earth.

As long as this "Cosmic Christianity" is understood as the cosmic intelligence of Michael that has *descended* to the earth in order to reveal the greater mysteries of Christ-Jesus, it is esoterically accurate. But when the truths of esoteric Christianity that have come down to the earth are hyperbolically *extended* back outwardly into the cosmos as something greater or superior to earth-based Christianity, then "Cosmic Christianity" becomes a Luciferic distortion.

The Luciferic distortion of anthroposophy is of course being actively resisted by the celestial and Rosicrucian overseers of anthroposophy; hence the crucial importance at this time to shine a strong literary spotlight on this insidious intrusion. In order to better understand and thereby counter the "Luciferization" of anthroposophy, the ancient pagan Mysteries (and Gnosticism) will here be examined in detail and then contrasted with the new "mysteries of the Son" as established by Christ-Jesus. The decayed remnants of the old Luciferic Mysteries that have survived in the various secret brotherhoods and in the Theosophical Society will also be critically examined in this study and contrasted with authentic esoteric Christianity as safeguarded and promulgated by the Rosicrucian Order and by true anthroposophical spiritual science.

CHAPTER 1

THE ANCIENT PAGAN MYSTERIES: THE LIGHT OF LUCIFERIC WISDOM DIES OUT

1.1 The Origin of the Pagan Mysteries

MANY PRESENT-DAY esoteric students very often display a wistful, yearning nostalgia concerning the arcane Mysteries of ancient times and a melancholic longing to re-establish them, or refound them, or renew them or rekindle them. The forlorn feeling is that it was a deep tragedy in human history when the ancient Mystery centres died out, taking with them their sublime secrets to the grave of time. Moreover, many esotericists are bitter and react quite angrily, blaming the rise of Christianity for their demise.

This reaction is not entirely surprising, considering that most esoteric students today were dedicated pupils of one or more of the old Mystery centres in previous lifetimes. Needless to say, these Mysteries have made quite a lasting impression on many souls.

Nevertheless, this longing to resurrect the dead Mysteries

runs counter to progressive human development and is based primarily on a false, foggy, rose-coloured misunderstanding of the nature of these Mysteries and the true reasons for their disappearance.

To begin with, all ancient Mysteries were initially established by supernatural beings far in advance of ordinary prehistoric humanity. These beings were members of a class of celestial evolution commonly referred to in Western culture as "angels." The angelic kingdom is one level above humanity in evolution, as humans are one level above the animal kingdom.

Some of the angel-beings who were the primordial teachers of prehistoric humanity, however, were not your ordinary angels. They had not fully completed their human-like stage of evolution on a previous planetary condition of the earth,[4] and hence were part angel and part human. In a sense, then, they were demi-angels or super-humans. When our present, mineralized earth condition came into planetary existence, these undeveloped angels were in an awkward situation: they needed further human experience but could not incarnate in physical human form since they were too far advanced. Their best solution was to work closely with prehistoric mankind as supernatural teachers and hopefully acquire the development they lacked.

While this all sounds benign and friendly enough, unfortunately for innocent mankind, these undeveloped angels were under the leadership of a far more advanced celestial being who had his own evolutionary agenda for humanity, vastly different from the divinely destined one. This being, known as Lucifer,[5] for long ages has intended to establish his own planetary sphere populated by ethereal human beings in an individualized soul condition of continuous dream-like fantasy. Blissfully somnolent humanity would of course be under Lucifer's direction and control for all time.

Though struggling humanity and the Luciferic angels mutually benefited from their ages-long interaction in the Mystery sanctuaries of antiquity, the human leaders were constantly at risk of being pulled away from earth existence by the luminous imaginations of Lucifer (the "Light-bearer") arising in the developing physical brain. Fortunately, humanity was kept grounded to the earth by the opposing action of the developed angels who faithfully worked under the close direction of their own highly advanced leader, Yahweh-Elohim.[6] Yahweh-Elohim and his progressive angels, as the subconscious instillers of tribal love, tethered mankind to the earth through the powerful forces of heredity.

However sublime was the knowledge received in the Mysteries of old, it was always bathed in a levitating, Luciferic light. The Light-bearer and his retrograde angels tirelessly strove to lead the pictorial thoughts of developing mankind away from the earth. Ironically, by developing the thinking powers of the physical brain, the resultant intellectual activity slowly extinguished mankind's instinctive clairvoyance of the supernatural, including perception of and contact with bright Lucifer and his angels.

1.2 The Temple Sleep

As humanity's dream-like awareness of the supernatural world slowly waned, the Mystery centres were forced to employ extraordinary measures in order to maintain some measure of conscious, supersensible perception and contact. The only remaining option was to place the initiate in a deep, cataleptic, near-death condition for three days, similar to a comatose patient under modern anesthetic. Such a procedure quite literally drove the initiate's soul from his body,[7] leaving only the thinnest thread of contact with the physical in order to prevent certain death. The difference with an anesthetically-induced coma and the "temple sleep" (as it was called) was that the initiate was lucid and aware of being out of the body and existing in the supernatural world. Remarkably, in this catatonic state the chief priest or "hierophant" (from the Greek "hierophántēs" meaning 'sacred revealer') was still able to direct the initiate's supernatural activity in a manner similar to today's technique of deep hypnotic suggestion.

While the closely-guarded body lay for three days in a death-like grip, the initiate of the pagan Mysteries was able to reconnect with supernatural beings and events, particularly the Luciferic angel guides, and recall this experience when carefully awakened by the temple priest. In this way, esoteric information was still obtained, particularly secrets of the plant and mineral kingdoms. Occasionally the pupil was able to contact more highly-advanced beings that were supersensibly connected with the other planets of the solar system, the highest of course being associated with the sun. Making contact with the Solar-Christos, the exalted leader of the sun, kept the influence of Lucifer and his angels in check since the sun-beings worked to promote humanity's destined evolutionary path of development.

Over time, even the hazardous technique of temple sleep no longer worked. Certain initiates could still be hypnotically placed in a much milder trance condition for a few hours and thereby impart information from the supernatural world when questioned by the priest; but they were no longer conscious of the experience and the information was much less reliable.

1.3   The Demise of the Ancient Mysteries

By the time the Jesus-child was born, the Mystery centres throughout the world were in desperate survival mode. The best they could do was to jealously guard whatever secret esoteric knowledge they had managed to retain from the past. This information was kept hidden from the profane in figurative form—in symbolic pictures, mythic stories, ritual ceremonies and dramatic performances. And over the course of later centuries, even the wisdom carefully locked up in symbolic form was lost to interpretation.

No amount of extraordinary resuscitation could revive the dying Mysteries. It wasn't Christianity that killed the pagan Mysteries; it was the march of human progress. Christ-Jesus came not to bury the old Mysteries or to salvage them. He came instead to establish an entirely new plan of salvation—to build up for all a new broad highway to heaven—not simply to reopen the old secretive path for the few that now trailed off into darkness.

For a time, the old pagan Mysteries served mankind well, but we should now respectfully let them rest in peace. Nostalgic attempts to dig them up and proudly trot around their decomposed remains serves no good purpose. Within the new mysteries established by Christ-Jesus can be found all the esoteric wisdom of the past[8] as well as sublime new wisdom never before revealed to human understanding that was beyond the reach of the old mysteries. Concerning himself in prophecy, Christ-Jesus stated: "I will utter secrets which have been kept secret from the foundation of the world" (Matt 13:35).

CHAPTER 2

GNOSTICISM:
THE GHOST OF MYSTERIES PAST

2.1   The Origin of Gnosticism

A SORROWFUL, roseate nostalgia, similar to the one felt towards the ancient Mysteries, also surrounds "Gnosticism" as it existed at the time of Christ-Jesus. Gnosticism can best be described as the discarnate, ideological ghost of the pagan Mysteries. As a short-lived, multi-assorted, loosely-defined movement, it was born out of the mystery idea of "gnosis"—experiential, esoteric wisdom that connected an initiate with the supernatural world.

   As Mystery centres closed down, certain fragments of the once secretly-guarded gnosis managed to escape with the displaced initiates. Lacking institutional control, this diminished esoteric wisdom seeded a profusion of exotic sects throughout the eastern Mediterranean and Middle East. The diverse scraps of esoteric wisdom that exhumed from the dying Mysteries in Egypt, Greece, Persia, Palestine and Roman Italy were very soon gathered into an entangled, gnostic potpourri of ideas.

Despite sectarian profusion and ideological diversity, Gnostic groups and individuals did share some fundamental beliefs. One was the pessimistic belief that that the entire universe was the flawed, evil creation of an inferior deity, given various names such as the Demiurge or Ialdabaoth. The Gnostic goal in life was to gain liberation from the dark realm of material existence and to rise above it into a region of supernal light, termed the "Pleroma." Liberation was achieved by possessing secret gnostic wisdom of the supernatural, by the application of certain magical formulae (called "theurgy") and occasionally by eliciting the help of a superhuman saviour known as "the Aeon Soter." Since the temple trance initiation of the old Mysteries no longer worked in most cases when Gnosticism appeared, this method of entry into supernatural reality was no longer a suitable salvific option.

2.2   Gnosticism versus Christianity

With the birth of Christianity, Gnosticism also attempted to incorporate some of the new theology into its negative worldview. Not surprisingly, Christian concepts were often distorted in novel, rather phantasmagoric ways. For example, the Gnostic Peretae sect integrated the notion of the Trinity; but in their belief, it was a trinity of the Father, Son and Hyle (the evil universe). The Son was also believed to be the serpent in paradise; in this case, a noble figure who rescued Eve from the dark clutches of Hyle. The Gnostic Sethians also held that the Trinitarian Son was the cosmic serpent associated with the biblical tree of knowledge of good and evil. Moreover, the Aeon Soter, who rescues the initiate from entrapment in Hyle, was easily equated with Christ-Jesus, the saviour of the world.

It was quite common among the diverse Gnostic sects, such as the Naasenes (from the Hebrew "nahas" meaning 'serpent'), to regard the serpent in a positive way, particularly as the foremost symbol of esoteric wisdom. It was likewise quite common in Gnostic circles, such as the Cainites, to regard the biblical Yahweh in a negative way, often equating him with the Demiurge, creator of the evil material world. The serpent of gnosis, then, was seen as a benefactor to humanity by saving the initiate from Yahweh's depraved material creation.

From these few examples, it is easy to see why Gnosticism, in general, incurred the wrath of condemnation from the early Church Fathers. Of course not every gnostic notion was inimical to early Christian theology; patristic philosopher Clement of Alexandria (c.150–c.215), for instance, made a distinction between heretical gnosis and genuine gnosis. Moreover, Gnostic writers were correct in associating the serpent with esoteric mystery wisdom; but the serpent is, of course, Lucifer and his retrograde angels since they were responsible for establishing the pagan Mystery centres. While primitive mankind certainly did benefit in many ways from Luciferic contact in the past, it also had dire, negative consequences to human evolution.

Since Gnosticism still retained some of the penetrating cosmology of the ancient Mysteries, it was still possible in the early years of Christianity to gain a faint glimmer of understanding concerning the celestial nature of Christ-Jesus and the complex process of his incarnation. Unfortunately this narrow porthole into the supernatural cosmos was soon submerged in a swirling concoction of pantheistic emanationism.[9] Immersion in Gnostic cosmology, such as that contained in the *Pistis Sophia*, is a complex and dizzying confusion of apocryphal beings: aeons, paralemptores, light maidens, heimarmene, spheres, realms of the midst, realms of the right and left and light treasures.

2.3   The Expiration of Gnosticism

As with the demise of the pagan Mysteries, there is a mistaken notion that intolerant Christianity was the cause of Gnosticism's rapid expiration. While intolerant church leaders were certainly feverishly opposed to heretical Gnosticism, the real cause of Gnostic dissolution was the evolutionary development of abstract intellectual reasoning that had begun around 600 BC. The rarified and intangible ideas of Gnosticism simply dissipated under the cold light of Aristotelian logic. The Age of Reason had begun and was beginning to relentlessly sweep away everything supernatural in its materialistic path.

There is a further mistaken notion that the exoteric church of conventional Christianity rigidified into authoritarian dogma because it rejected and failed to include Gnosticism and Mystery wisdom, and therefore lacked a vivifying, esoteric component. This common error is based primarily on misunderstanding the true mission of exoteric Christianity; which is to provide a more basic, alternate stream of Christian teaching that is complementary but distinct from esoteric Christianity. The doctrine of repeated earth-lives (reincarnation), for example, was not to be taught in the exoteric Church,[10] though it was known and understood within the Johannine stream of esoteric Christianity. Besides, mainstream Christianity was not left barren of any esoteric component, since that would certainly have resulted in serious religious rigidification. The path of Mystic-Christianity contained particularly within the Gospel of St. John was practiced and nurtured within the various monastic orders and by numerous influential mystics and visionaries of the Church such as St. John of the Cross, St. Catherine of Siena and St. Teresa of Avila.

The Luciferic knowledge that characterized the old pagan Mysteries and Gnosticism was not preserved and perpetuated in its original form within the new mysteries of esoteric Christianity. The new mysteries of the Son, established by Christ-Jesus himself, are of a much higher order and completely supersede all the mystery knowledge that came before.

CHAPTER 3

THE LIGHT OF THE
NEW CHRISTIAN MYSTERIES:
THE DIVINE LIFE OF CHRIST-JESUS

3.1 The Mysteries of Christ-Jesus and the Pagan Mysteries

IT'S FUNDAMENTALLY important to understand how vastly different the new mysteries of Christ-Jesus are from the old Luciferic mysteries that came before. A good place to start is perhaps with a familiar analogy: the difference between the sun and the moon. The moon does not radiate light of its own, but rather reflects the light of the sun. In the process, the sunlight is diminished and transformed; it becomes polarized light. The sun, on the other hand, powerfully radiates its own full spectrum of light which is the source of all physical life on earth.

Analogously, the pagan mysteries were quite literally moon-wisdom. The supersensible sphere of activity for the present-day angels extends from the earth to the orbit of the moon. For this reason, and the fact that the ordinary angels completed their human level of evolution (the attainment of self-conscious awareness) during the Ancient Moon period of planetary development, angels are often referred to in esoteric literature as "moon beings," "lunar ancestors" or "lunar pitris."

Lucifer, together with his angels, and Yahweh, together with his angels, assisted prehistoric humanity in their early development; but in significantly different ways. The moon beings led by Yahweh faithfully reflected the powerful evolutionary impulses radiating from the more advanced beings of the sun. The moon beings led by Lucifer distortedly reflected the higher cosmic wisdom for their own purposes; so in a true sense, Luciferic knowledge was a diminished, polarized moon-wisdom.

All ancient supernatural knowledge, then, was not exclusively Luciferic moon-wisdom. Through the psychological cohesion of tribal love and the physiological fastening of tribal heredity, Yahweh and his progressive moon angels were able to "raise up a chosen people"—the ancient Hebrews—and morally instruct them through an established priesthood and through prophetical leaders such as Moses. As a result, the human soul in ancient times was often the arena for a supernatural tug-of-war between the two classes of moon beings.

In rare instances, beings more advanced than either of the two classes of lunar angels had established wisdom sanctuaries in the past, particularly on ancient Atlantis; the foremost was, not surprisingly, the sun-oracle. These centres did not survive individually after the Great Flood, but were consolidated into one major esoteric centre that was geographically situated for a time in central Asia.[11] Shambhala, as it was known in Tibet, was first established by an advanced Atlantean initiate of the sun-oracle, called Manu.[12]

3.2 Christ-Jesus and Shambhala

Shambhala, as a sanctuary of sun-wisdom, similar to the Mystery centres of moon-wisdom, also exhibited a two-fold division; but in this case, it was based not so much on knowledge possessed, but on level of attainment. The inner circle of Shambhala was comprised of twelve exceedingly advanced beings known in the East as "bodhisattvas" and in the West as the "masters of wisdom and harmony of feelings." The outer circle was comprised of highly-developed initiate followers who were at a level of development below that of the bodhisattvas.

In antediluvian times, the twelve bodhisattva beings that were responsible for sanctuaries of sun-wisdom were from an evolutionary stream one step above the angels. These beings are known in the West as "archangels." Over the long ages, the archangelic bodhisattva leaders have gradually been replaced by human initiates who have remarkably progressed beyond ordinary humanity to the level of archangels.

Though the human bodhisattvas no longer need to physically incarnate for their own development, they have willingly chosen to continue to do so in order to materially assist Christ-Jesus in his salvational work for mankind. This free, self-sacrificial decision is known as the "bodhisattva vow." It is only when a bodhisattva rises to the level of a buddha, as occurred with Siddhartha Gautama, that the decision is made to no longer physically incarnate. However, this does not mean that an advanced initiate at the level of buddhahood no longer cares about or works with humanity; only that their continued assistance is directed entirely from the supersensible realm.

Throughout the ages, the human bodhisattvas of Shambhala have provided mankind with radiant bursts of sun-wisdom to also counterbalance the Luciferic moon-wisdom of the Mysteries. Many of the founders of the ancient major religions were incarnated bodhisattvas, such as Zarathustra (the founder of Persian Zoroastrianism) and Siddhartha Gautama (the founder of Buddhism). Zarathustra directed religious attention to Ahura Mazda, the deity of the sun; Gautama Buddha was the first to embody for humanity the great truths of peace and compassion.

Historically, Shambhala and the illustrious masters of sun-wisdom have remained deeply hidden from ordinary humanity; not because of elitism, but in order to quietly work behind the scenes of human development so as not to attract unwanted attention. Since mankind is destined to increasingly develop conscious free-will, it is exceedingly important that these advanced individuals not unduly affect the course of human events by their powerful presence in public or on the world stage. Occasionally, if the seriousness of world affairs warrants it, a master of the sun will appear in public for a brief time, such as occurred prior to the French Revolution with the legendary Count of Saint- Germain.

The once geographical sanctuary of Shambhala has also been protected from the profane public scrutiny of modern times by being raised to a supernatural level. It currently exists as an etheric sphere encircling the earth. Moreover, since the incarnation of Christ-Jesus, the heart of Shambhala is no longer situated above the ancient sacred island in the Gobi, but in the supersensible atmosphere above Jerusalem, the new "Christ-centre of the world."

Even though the sun-wisdom that radiated from the ancient centre of Shambhala was far loftier and more elevated than the moon-wisdom of the Mysteries, it was still just a candle glow when compared to the resplendent glory of the new Christian mysteries—the mysteries of the Son—that now radiate from Christ-Jesus himself, who is supersensibly centred in the sacred heart of Shambhala, the "New Jerusalem."

3.3   Christ-Jesus *is* the Mystery

When using the word "mystery" today, it is fundamentally important to understand that it has a much more transcendent meaning with the Christian mysteries than it had with the Luciferic mysteries. In the pagan mysteries, the word meant secret rites and knowledge concerning the supernatural world that was accessible only to the initiated few. The human leaders of the old mysteries conveyed objective knowledge *about* supernatural beings, and the highest attainable initiatory experience was to obtain objective knowledge *about* the celestial leader of the sun. In order to acquire this supernatural gnosis, the soul of the initiate had to be artificially ejected from the physical body for at least three days.

With Christianity, however, the word mystery does not mean hidden secrets guarded for the initiated few. A mystery in the Christian sense *only* pertains to the ineffable nature of God. While God can certainly be known and experienced, the complete fullness of his eternal and infinite nature is logically beyond any temporal and finite mind to contain. The Trinity, then, is a Christian "mystery," not because it is secret, but because it pertains to the nature of God and is therefore not completely comprehensible to the human mind. Though God can be increasingly understood and known throughout the course of time, his transcendent nature will always remain something of a mystery to the human mind.

Mystery in Christian terminology, then, does not mean something completely unknowable. The divine nature continually strives to reveal itself to human understanding; that is, to make "know[n] the mysteries of the kingdom of heaven" (Matt 13:11) to all who sincerely seek them. The Christian mysteries are not concerned with keeping secrets, but in revealing and understanding the hidden wisdom of God in all things. As Christ-Jesus has clearly stated in scripture: "For nothing is hid that shall not be made manifest, nor anything secret that shall not be known and come to light" (Lk 8:17).

Since the divine nature was incarnated in Christ-Jesus, the key to understanding the new mysteries, whether greater or lesser, is that the Messiah didn't come to re-establish another Mystery religion, he *is* the divine mystery! The new mysteries are not about contacting divinity by *leaving* the confines of the earth through the dangerous doorway of a secret trance; but about experiencing and comprehending the divine nature that *came* to earth, in full view for all to behold. To understand Christ-Jesus is to understand the entire cosmos. Moreover, extraordinary and life-threatening techniques are no longer required to contact the Solar-Christos in the supernatural world. Since the foremost leader of the sun was intimately involved in the consummate process of uniting the human and the divine, he is now freely accessible through the Christian mysteries.

It cannot be emphasized enough that Christ-Jesus came not to *create* more mysteries guarded in secret, but to *be* a mystery open to the world. Christ-Jesus came not to *convey* divine revelations, but to *be* a divine revelation. By the very fact of his divine nature, every aspect of the life of Christ-Jesus *is* a divine mystery. Therefore, his birth is a mystery; his words are a mystery; his death is a mystery; his resurrection is a mystery.

Through his divine nature, Christ-Jesus is "the way, the truth and the life." He is, then, more than a mere teacher of mystery truth; he *is* the mystery truth that he teaches. He is more than a mere way-shower of a mystery path; he *is* the mystery way that he shows. He is more than simply living a spiritual life in the mysteries; he *is* the mystery life of the spirit.

The mysteries connected to the divine life of Christ-Jesus have been entrusted to both exoteric Christianity and to esoteric Christianity. The lesser and greater mysteries do not indicate different mysteries, or a superiority of mysteries, but rather the manner in which these mysteries are pursued and understood. The greater mysteries, then, go into greater supersensible detail and complexity regarding the life of Christ-Jesus; the lesser mysteries go into lesser supersensible detail and complexity regarding the life of Christ-Jesus. It is important to be clear, however, that both approaches are equally demanding, profound and illuminating. Any mystery, greater or lesser concerning the life of Christ-Jesus, will affect us deeply: it will revivify our bodies, sanctify our souls and leave our own lives transformed through supernatural grace.

Twenty mysteries connected to the life of Christ-Jesus have been helpfully delineated and arranged in the Catholic practice of the rosary: five joyful mysteries, five sorrowful mysteries, five glorious mysteries and five luminous mysteries. Since every aspect of the divine life of Christ-Jesus is an infinite mystery, there is of course no limit to the number of mysteries that can be intellectually delineated and devoutly pursued.

CHAPTER 4

THE BURIED CORPSE
OF THE OLD MYSTERIES:
SECRET BROTHERHOODS IN THE
MIDDLE EAST, EUROPE AND AMERICA

4.1   The Rise of Muhammadanism

WHEN THE ANCIENT Mysteries could no longer directly connect with the supernatural realm, either through atavistic clairvoyance or through trance initiation, then effectively the life went out these religious institutions. At the time of Christ-Jesus, the Mysteries were an institutional body without a soul. What was left were the ideologically mummified remains of esoteric knowledge encased in a secret sarcophagus of abstruse symbols, elaborate rituals, dramatic mythic presentations and cryptic magical formulae.

Though the dead Mysteries as respected and influential institutions were socially, culturally and religiously buried in later Roman times, their slowly decomposing remains were nevertheless preserved by a few faithful initiates and distributed piecemeal over the centuries throughout the

Middle East, Europe and then later in America.

In time, the displaced initiates and their successors attracted small groups of followers and re-formed themselves into small religious sects and secret brotherhoods in order to perpetuate the dusty ashes of dead Mystery knowledge.

In the Middle East, with the rapid rise of Muhammadanism during the early centuries of Christianity, any secret sects or brotherhoods that were newly established became well-hidden to European eyes beneath obscuring layers of Muslim culture and society. Any vestiges of the old mystery wisdom were usually merged with the widespread, dominant Islamic teachings.

During the tenth century, the devotees of one such esoteric Islamic sect, known as the Batinis, believed there was a hidden inner meaning to sacred texts, rituals and religious prescriptions ("batini") that was understandable only to the initiated few; as opposed to an outer level of meaning ("zahiri") that was comprehensible to the broad masses.

Another esoteric Muslim sect founded in the eleventh century, the Druze, also maintained the characteristic mystery-style division between a smaller group of initiates (known as "al-'Uqqāl": the 'knowledgeable initiates') who had access to their sacred literature and special gatherings; and a larger group of secular followers (known as "al-Juhhāl": the 'ignorant') who did not have access to the sacred literature or the special gatherings.

Islamic mystics, known as Sufis (from the Greek "sophia": 'wisdom'), traditionally traced their beginnings back to Muhammad himself (570–632) who was believed to have transmitted an esoteric gnosis; that is, direct experiential wisdom of God, to an inner circle of prepared followers. This Islamic gnosis was said to have been orally passed down from teacher to pupil until it became partially summarized during the early Middle Ages in manuals such as *Al-Risâla* (al-Shafi'I; c.1045).

During the first millennium, throughout the Middle East, there was also a profusion of secret Islamic sects that were far less esoteric and much more overtly political and militant, the most famous of course being the Hashishin, known popularly as the "Order of Assassins." The founder of this secret society of deadly mercenaries, the grandmaster of the order, was Hasan-i-Sabbah (c.1050–1124). Sabbah headquartered his Order in the ancient fortress at Alamut in northwestern Iran, and was referred to in the accounts of Marco Polo as the "Old Man of the Mountain."

4.2 European Mystery Centres

In medieval Europe, as exoteric Christianity rapidly spread and replaced the numerous indigenous pagan beliefs, the old Mystery centres also closed their doors. What is quite remarkable, however, was that the vast majority of European initiates willingly renounced the ancient institutions and readily embraced esoteric Christianity. There are two primary reasons for this seemingly unexpected occurrence.

The first is that the various European mysteries were associated with the northern migration of the illustrious Atlantean sun-initiate, Manu, to the Shambhala sanctuary in Central Asia.[14] As such, many of the esoteric European centres celebrated a supernatural connection to the Solar-Christos through certain sun mysteries. Therefore, even at a geographical distance they had already been clairvoyantly aware of certain monumental events that took place in the life of Christ-Jesus on earth. By the time early Christian missionaries arrived in barbarian Europe, the northern initiates had already been preparing for profound esoteric change.

The second reason for the sudden acceptance of esoteric Christianity by the initiates of the European Mysteries is that after the ascension of Christ-Jesus, the archangelic guiding spirit of the northern Germanic and Celtic peoples—the Celtic folk soul—willingly became the supernatural sponsor of esoteric Christianity. In the words of Rudolf Steiner:

> [T]he Archangel of the Celtic peoples … became the inspirer of esoteric Christianity. All the underlying teachings and impulses of esoteric Christianity, especially of the real, true esoteric Christianity, have their source in his inspirations. (*The Mission of the Folk Souls in Relation to Teutonic Mythology*; Lecture 11 given in 1910)

As a result, pre-Christian initiates such as the Arthurian Knights of the Round Table easily morphed into the medieval Knights of the Holy Grail. The sacred cauldron of Celtic myth, such as the large magical cauldron in the Welsh story of *Branwen, Daughter of Llyr* that revivified warriors newly-killed in battle, easily transformed into the chalice of the Holy Grail that contained the secret of eternal life. The magic cauldron warmed by the breath of nine maidens in the Welsh poem, *The Spoils of Annwn*, which King Arthur had to retrieve by undertaking a perilous journey by ship to Annwn, the Welsh underworld, effortlessly became the formidable Quest for the Holy Grail.

Dusty remnants of the pagan mysteries of the Middle East, particularly from Egypt, were also secretly carried into medieval Europe in some rather interesting ways. Though the exact historical details continue to be shrouded in fanciful conjecture, many Western esotericists have long held that the symbolism of the tarot cards, particularly the major arcana, can be directly traced back to ancient Egypt. Certainly by the time they publicly appeared in various parts of Europe in the fifteenth century, the original symbolic pictures had become somewhat Westernized. Nevertheless, it is believed that the symbolic images are corrupted fragments of the Egyptian Book of Thoth, secretly brought to Europe by the gypsies.

The word "gypsy" derives from the Greek word for "Egypt." As related by Manley P. Hall in *The Secret Teachings of All Ages* (1928):

> A curious legend relates that after the destruction of the Serapeum in Alexandria, the large body of attendant priests banded themselves together to preserve the secrets of the rites of Serapis. Their descendants (Gypsies) carrying with them the most precious of the volumes saved from the burning library—the Book of Enoch, or Thoth (the Tarot)—became wanderers upon the face of the earth, remaining a people apart with an ancient language and a birthright of magic and mystery.

4.3   The Medieval Brotherhood of Stonemasons

Another curious repository in medieval Europe of antiquated pagan mystery wisdom, particularly ancient Hebrew and Egyptian, was within the brotherhood of stonemasons. Not surprisingly, since this brotherhood has been a guarded fraternity for centuries (even to its own members), public records concerning its past history are scarce. Besides, what remained of the old mysteries after their disappearance in the first centuries after Christ-Jesus was entirely in the form of symbolic imagery, ritual, myth and drama—not written documents.

So, how was it that a medieval guild of hardworking labourers and craftsmen became such an influential storehouse of ancient mystery wisdom? The answer really is quite simple. Think of all the wondrous, awe-inspiring religious, civic and military structures of the past: the pyramids of Egypt, the stone circles of Britain, the temples of Greece, the forum buildings of Rome, the fortresses of the Crusaders, the castles of Europe and the cathedrals of the Church. All of these massive ancient superstructures were built of stone, and someone had to conceive, engineer and construct them.

Stonemasons, particularly the master masons, were exceedingly skilled and talented, much in demand, and held in high esteem throughout ancient and medieval times. Rulers, priests and military generals could not survive without them. Without masterful shapers of stone, ancient civilization as we know it would not have existed.

Even today, the technological expertise of architectural construction is based on the acquired skills, experience and know-how that has been learned and retained from prior generations. Otherwise, builders would quite literally be required to continually "re-invent the wheel." Not surprisingly then, medieval stonemasons could trace the illustrious history of their trade, their "craft," back through the long centuries to the glorious civilizations of the past. Echoes of the mystery wisdom that inspired the ancient immortal monuments in stone were proudly passed down from generation to generation of stonemasons, not through written records but through symbolic carvings, pictorial illustrations, word-of-mouth and memory.

Some Masonic legends even trace the history of the Craft back as far as Enoch, the eldest son of Cain, who lived before the Great Flood. As described by M. P. Hall:

> According to Freemasonic symbolism, Enoch, fearing that all knowledge of the sacred Mysteries would be lost at the time of the Deluge, erected … two columns … Upon the metal column in appropriate allegorical symbols he engraved the secret teaching and upon the marble column placed an inscription stating that a short distance away a priceless treasure would be discovered in a subterranean vault. After having thus faithfully completed his labors, Enoch was translated from the brow of Mount Moriah. In time the location of the secret vaults was lost, but after the lapse of ages there came another builder—an initiate after

the order of Enoch—and he, while laying the foundations for another temple to the Great Architect of the Universe, discovered the long-lost vaults and the secrets contained within. (Ibid)

In feudal times, two-thirds of Europe's population lived in serfdom, basically as slaves of the wealthy aristocratic landowners. A serf, however, could earn his freedom by working a year and a day at some trade such as stonemasonry. By becoming "freemasons," feudal labourers gained increased prosperity, prestige, independence and social mobility. Moreover, by uniting together in a strong guild, the masonic labourer had increased bargaining power on construction projects. By the middle of the thirteenth century, the strong bond of brotherhood had resulted in lodges becoming established on every construction site at the patron's expense.

Lodges were at the heart of masonic life: they were schools, dormitories, dining facilities, banks, libraries, lounges, meeting halls and warehouses. Since the lodges carefully stored the freemasons' collective wealth and their "trade secrets"; that is, their specialized tools and detailed architectural drawings that were essential to their livelihood, entrance had to be carefully guarded with a system of secret knocks, passwords and handshakes.

The complexities of Gothic stone construction also required a graded system of training involving three levels of advancement: entered apprentice, fellow craft and master mason. In order to become a freemason, a candidate needed to be initiated into the brotherhood with a special ceremony, and progression through the three degrees involved further ritualized induction. These rituals would incorporate the arcane traditions of the remote past to impress upon the Freemasonic member "pride of profession"; that is, belonging to an august brotherhood with a long, proud and distinguished history.

Throughout the Middle Ages, the brotherhood of

freemasons grew to be a united and powerful workers' society, stronger than any other guild at the time. Membership was entirely comprised of operative stonemasons; that is, practicing tradesmen actively labouring at the craft of stone building. After the fourteenth century, however, with the rising tide of the Renaissance Age, membership in the brotherhood would fundamentally and radically change.

4.4   The Rise of Speculative Freemasonry

As the Feudal Age was coming to an end, there were of course fewer and fewer stone fortresses, stone castles and stone cathedrals being built throughout Europe. Consequently, the noble craft of Freemasonry also went into a slow decline. Remarkably, however, as the number of operative stonemasons diminished in the brotherhood due to decreased occupational demand, there was also a corresponding increase in the number of members who were not skilled tradesmen and who did not even practice the craft of stonemasonry. These non-operative or "speculative" masons were very often wealthy, highly-educated aristocrats and noblemen. By the time the Grand Lodge of England was formally established in 1717, almost all of the various European brotherhoods were composed of non-practicing, speculative masons. So how did this strange turn of events occur, and what effect did this have on the atavistic mystery wisdom incorporated in the brotherhood?

As the overall architects, engineers and labour managers of an ambitious stone construction, such as a castle or cathedral, the master masons necessarily had close contact with the wealthy patrons of the project. On occasion, these patrons would be invited to the masonic lodge for planning sessions, construction meetings or simply as invited guests. Their attendance would of course lend increased prestige to the brotherhood's reputation with the other feudal guilds.

On rare occasions, as honorary guests, these wealthy patrons would be invited to observe some of the arcane induction ceremonies that were secretly held for masonic members within the lodge. Not surprisingly, these age-old rituals very often made a deep and lasting impression on the aristocratic guests; so much so that in time a few agreed to undergo the masonic inductions themselves to become honorary master masons of the craft (similar to today's university practice of conferring honorary degrees on noteworthy individuals).

The masonic aspects of secrecy and ritual understandably appealed to wealthy statesmen, generals and judges who were used to maintaining state secrets, military secrets or judicial secrets; and who also enjoyed elaborate pomp, ceremony and regalia in their official duties. Once membership in the Freemasonic brotherhood became socially fashionable for the wealthy, even royalty decided to join. According to Mackey's *Encyclopedia of Freemasonry* (1909), there is good historical evidence that royalty was seriously involved in the British brotherhoods as far back as 926, when Prince Edwin, the brother of Anglo-Saxon king Athelstan, convened as grand master a general assembly of freemasons at York. A code of laws was allegedly adopted, which is said to be the basis for all subsequent Masonic constitutions. As recorded in the Masonic *Book of Constitutions* (James Anderson; 1738):

> [A]ccordingly Prince Edwin summoned all the Free and Accepted Masons in the Realm, to meet him in the Congregation at York, who came and formed the Grand Lodge under him as their Grand Master, AD. 926.
>
> That they brought with them many old Writings and Records of the Craft, some in Greek, some in Latin some in French, and other languages; and from the contents thereof, they framed the Constitutions of the English

Lodges, and made a Law for themselves, to preserve and observe the same in all Time coming.

Anderson also indicated that some written records were even in existence prior to this time but were destroyed:

> That though the Ancient records of the Brotherhood in England were most of them destroyed or lost in the war with the Danes, who burnt the Monasteries where the Records were kept. (Ibid)

Once the wealthy, the powerful and the well-educated became involved, they quickly assumed control of the brotherhoods; but of course entirely along nationalistic lines. British Freemasonry (Grand Lodge), for example, was strictly opposed to (or in the language of the Craft, "did not have amity with") French Freemasonry (Grand Orient). At this point in history, Freemasonry became "establishment," and social standing, prestige and advancement became crucially dependent on belonging to a Freemasonic lodge. Freemasonry became essentially a secretive "old boy's club," a covert means to acquire and maintain political, social and economic power in the hands of the few.

This of course is not to say that there haven't been sincere, honest, upright and honourable members of the Craft over the last three centuries; only that within the already secretive body of ordinary Masons, there are elite inner circles of powerful initiates whose membership is tightly controlled and whose dealings are completely unknown to the ordinary members. In addition to the three lower degrees in ordinary Craft Masonry that are governed by a grand lodge, there is an extended system of thirty higher degrees that are governed by an entirely separate organization, a supreme council. In this hidden Masonry, membership is highly exclusive since access to the top fifteen degrees, particularly the thirty-third (33°) degree, is decided strictly by the unanimous consent of the ruling supreme council. An international network of supreme councils ensures that Masonic decisions and control remains in the hands of a powerful few.[15]

Once Freemasonry had become an integral component of the British establishment, it rapidly spread to all corners of the earth as a colonial feature of the British Commonwealth. It took particular root in the socially experimental soil of America. By 1752, George Washington had been properly initiated into the brotherhood. With the signing of the Declaration of Independence, eight signatories were proven Masons, including Benjamin Franklin and John Hancock, as well as twenty-four others who were alleged to be Masons. In the nineteenth century, Masonic membership exploded due essentially to the willing recruitment from the burgeoning middle and professional classes who regarded the brotherhood as a sure door to success and social advancement.

4.5   The Paganization of Freemasonry

The most astounding development of Freemasonry from the Renaissance to today is that in the process of shaking off all occupational association with operative stonemasonry and becoming entirely a secret society of speculative initiates, the brotherhood succeeded in unearthing the deteriorated corpse of the old pagan mysteries. As long as the expired remnants of the pagan mysteries were subsumed as symbolic history in a workingman's craft, they were not harmful or regressive. Besides, medieval stonemasons were Christian, and any elements of pagan wisdom were safely balanced and contained by regular participation in the Catholic Mass.

By gradually de-Christianizing medieval Freemasonry in the eighteenth century, the skeletal remains of the old pagan mysteries were exhumed and dressed up. While all of the fourteenth-century English masonic regulations, known as the Old Charges, were specifically Christian and while the majority of them expressed loyalty to the Holy Church, in the *Ancient Masonic Constitutions* of 1723 (James Anderson) the only mention of Christ-Jesus occurs once in the preamble. Moreover, any belief in the Trinitarian God of Christianity was replaced by a general Voltarian deism,[16] as indicated in the first of the new "Charges of a Free-Mason" which stated: "['T]is now thought more expedient only to oblige them [Freemasons] to that Religion to which all men agree, leaving their particular opinions to themselves." This impersonal deity which Masons were "obliged" to believe was known as "The Great Architect of the Universe," or simply "TGAOTU."

Stephen Knight in *The Brotherhood: The Secret World of the Freemasons* (2007) provided the following additional historical detail regarding the paganization of Freemasonry:

> [T]he process of transformation of the old masons' guild continued. The brotherhood was de-Christianized and the rituals of the various workings [degrees] became formalized. Throughout the eighteenth century more and more pagan elements were brought in to replace the discarded faith … The main rituals settled around the legend of King Solomon's temple. The myth mimed in the Master Mason's degree is the murder of Hiram Abiff, claimed to have been the principal architect of the temple, for refusing to reveal Masonic secrets. The would-be Master Mason has to 'die' as Hiram Abiff and be 'resurrected' into Masonry.

Though the seemingly neutral term for God, "The Great Architect of the Universe," had been widely used by even prominent Christian writers such as St. Thomas Aquinas, it was not without pagan associations; most notably, the Gnostic malevolent Demiurge was also called the Great Architect of the Universe. Any doubt regarding the inclusion of a pagan god in the secret mysteries of Freemasonry was removed at the fourth degree, known as the Holy Royal Arch Degree of the "Secret Master." In this particular ritual of initiation ("exaltation"), the "omnific word"—the lost sacred and mysterious name of God—was revealed to the master Mason as "JAH BUL ON": a composite of Yah = Yahweh; Bul = Baal; and On = Osirus. Since Baal was the false god of the Old Testament and Osirus was the Egyptian god of the underworld, Jahbulon clearly represented a pre-Christian, pagan deity.[17]

The average Freemason of today, particularly in the three lower degrees, knows almost nothing of the extensive pagan mysteries contained within the symbolic architecture, the mythical ceremonies, the allegorical initiations, the representational regalia and the figurative language of their secretive brotherhood.[18] But a great many initiate brothers of the higher degrees know plenty. They are well aware, for example, that Freemasonry has become a pale and faded perpetuation of the ancient Mysteries. Albert Pike 33° (1809–1891), the Illustrious Sovereign Grand Commander of the Supreme Council of Charleston, USA (also referred to as the "Mother Supreme Council of the World"), stated this knowledge clearly in the classic Masonic manual *Morals and Dogma* (1871):

> [T]he mysteries, of which Masonry is the legitimate successor—from the earliest times the custodian and depository of the great philosophical and religious truths, unknown to the world at large, and handed down from age to age by an unbroken current of tradition, embodied in symbols, emblems, and allegories … Masonry is identical to the ancient Mysteries.

As well, Manly P. Hall 33° (1901–1990), in *The Lost Keys of Freemasonry of the Secret of Hiram Abiff* (1923) is equally clear:

The true Masonic Lodge is a Mystery School ... [A]ncient mystic teachings as perpetuated in the modern rites are sacred, and that powers unseen and unrecognized mold the destiny of those who consciously and of their own free will take upon themselves the obligations of the Fraternity ... [A]ncient Freemasonry and the beautiful cosmic allegories that it teaches, perpetuated through hundreds of lodges and ancient mysteries, forms the oldest of the Mystery Schools; and its preservation through the ages has not depended upon itself as an exoteric body of partly evolved individuals but upon a concealed brotherhood.

4.6   Freemasonry and Lucifer

High-level Masons such as Pike and Hall also understand, maintain and celebrate the luminous supernatural source of pagan mystery wisdom—Lucifer. As with the Gnostic serpent, Lucifer is held in high Masonic esteem as the great benefactor of mankind. He's the promethean light-bearer whose wisdom-fire stolen from the gods dispels the dark gloom of human ignorance. Since Masonry is regarded as the modern-day heir to the throne of the Mysteries, Lucifer is rightfully its sovereign lord. In the "Instructions" of Grand Commander Albert Pike that were addressed to the 23 supreme councils of the world on July 14, 1889, he stated:

To you, Sovereign Grand Inspectors General, we say this, that you may repeat it to the Brethren of the 32nd, 31st and 30th degrees—The Masonic religion should be, by all of us initiates of the high degrees, maintained in the of purity of the Luciferian doctrine.
    If Lucifer were not God, would Adonay whose deeds prove his cruelty, perfidy, and hatred of man, barbarism and repulsion for science, would Adonay and his priests, calumniate him?

Yes, Lucifer is God, and unfortunately Adonay is also God. For the eternal law is that there is no light without shade, no beauty without ugliness, no white without black, for the absolute can only exist as two Gods: darkness being necessary to light to serve as its foil as the pedestal is necessary to the statue, and the brake to the locomotive.

Thus, the doctrine of Satanism is a heresy; and the true and pure philosophic religion is the belief in Lucifer, the equal of Adonay; but Lucifer, God of Light and God of Good, is struggling for humanity against Adonay, the God of Darkness and Evil.[19]

We can see from this quotation that Pike makes a distinction between Lucifer and Satan, praising the "God of Light" and condemning the "God of Darkness." Modern-day Masonic apologists are quite correct in stating that they're not Satan worshippers, but knowingly or unknowingly they are initiate disciples in the new lodge of Lucifer.

"Masonry's greatest philosopher," Manly P. Hall, also wrote that the true God of Light, the "light of the Lodge," is the serpent-king Lucifer; and that the high-level master Mason becomes a willing communicator of Luciferic knowledge:

The glorious privileges of a Master Mason are in keeping with his greater knowledge and wisdom ... For him the heavens have opened and the Great Light has bathed him in its radiance ... The Prodigal Son, so long a wanderer in the regions of darkness, has returned to his Father's house. The voice speaks from the Heavens, its power thrilling the Master until his own being seems filled with its divinity, saying, 'This is my beloved Son, in whom I am well pleased' ... The Master Mason is in truth a sun, a great reflector of light, who radiates through his organism, purified by ages of preparation, the glorious power which is the light of the Lodge. He, in truth, has become the spokesman of the Most High. He stands between the glowing fire light and the world. Through him passes Hydra, the great snake, and from its mouth there pours to man the light of God. (*The Lost Keys of Freemasonry*)

Furthermore, according to Hall the perfected master Mason is also able to acquire immense Luciferic power as well as "glorious" Luciferic light:

The day has come when Fellow Craftsmen must know and apply their knowledge. The lost key to their grade is the mastery of emotion, which places the energy of the universe at their disposal. Man can only expect to be entrusted with great power by proving his ability to use it constructively and selflessly. When the Mason learns that the key to the warrior on the block is the proper application of the dynamo of living power, he has learned the mystery of his Craft. The seething energies of Lucifer are in his hands and before he may step onward and upward, he must prove his ability to properly apply energy. (Ibid)

Fortunately in this case, in the evolutionary course of abstract intellectual development, as human beings gradually lost clairvoyant access to the supernatural realm, they also lost the ability to willfully access and apply powerful supernatural forces. While forms of black magic continue to exist today, they are mere child's play compared to the horrific misapplication of supernatural forces on ancient Atlantis. Befriending Lucifer in modern Freemasonry does more psychological harm to the individual soul than it does external damage to the world and to others.

The fact that today's Masonic ritual survives simply as a piteous, hollowed-out remnant of ancient Mystery practices that once had supernatural effectiveness is no better exemplified than in the initiatory "raising of a master Mason from death to life" in the lodge. In Freemasonry, the initiate is no longer placed in an actual stone sarcophagus for three days in a deep cataleptic trance where his immortal soul is separated from his mortal body to traverse the supernatural realm and to return transformed as a true "knower" of cosmic mysteries. Instead of an actual stone sepulcher, the Masonic initiate is ritually placed on a large cloth on the floor with the design of a full-size coffin, including skull and crossbones, symbolically placed on it. Instead of the temple trance, the Masonic initiate is simply blindfolded; and instead of being comatose for three days, the ritually-dead initiate is carried around the inside of the lodge room three times. Rather than being reawakened from the prolonged death-like trance by the hierophant of the Mystery temple, the Masonic initiate is simply raised to a standing position after lying on the floor by the worshipful master of the lodge who uses a special hand grip called the "lion's paw." Hardly the life-altering sojourn in the supernatural realm that was once experienced by the initiate of the ancient Mysteries.

Nevertheless, despite its esoteric destitution, Freemasonry has indeed been the "mother lodge of the world," spawning countless imitations—a worldwide profusion of secret brotherhoods—all modeled in some way on the Freemasonic template. Hundreds of secret brotherhoods as diverse as the philanthropic Independent Order of Odd Fellows, and the Mormon inner priesthood known as the Order of Melchizedek, to the notorious Ordo Templi Orientis (O.T.O.), all have firm occult roots in mother Masonry.

Mainstream Christianity has for centuries been well aware of non-operative Freemasonry's connection to the old pagan Mysteries. The first papal condemnation occurred in 1738, which was further upheld and reinforced in 1884 by Pope Leo XIII in his famous encyclical *Humanum Genus*. Likewise, the Lutheran, Methodist and Presbyterian communities later declared Freemasonry to be incompatible with Christianity. The Greek Orthodox Church in 1933 formally condemned

Freemasonry on the clear understanding that "it constitutes a mystagogical system which reminds us of the ancient heathen mystery-religions and cults—from which it descends and is their continuation and regeneration." Surprisingly, however, according to Stephen Knight "The Church of England has been a stronghold of Freemasonry for more than two hundred years. Traditionally, joining the brotherhood and advancing within it has always been the key to preferment in the [Anglican] Church." (*The Brotherhood*)

4.7   The Riddle of the Knights Templar

It is worth clarifying, at this point, the ever-popular misconception that the Knights Templar also functioned as an important esoteric conduit into medieval Europe for the vanishing mysteries of the ancient Middle East. As a Christian, monastic, military order officially endorsed by the Catholic Church at the Council of Troyes in 1129, the Templar mission was to provide protection to European pilgrims travelling at that time to Jerusalem and to the Holy Land. Templar knights were required to take the monastic vows of poverty, chastity, piety and obedience, and to strictly adhere to a detailed code of conduct known as the "Latin Rule" which was established by advocate St. Bernard of Clairvaux and founder Hugues de Payens.

Though the Templars certainly came into armed contact with militant Moslem brotherhoods such as the Order of Assassins, as a fervent and dedicated Christian order, they had no interest in becoming a secret repository for old pagan mystery knowledge. However, since the Order's headquarters in Jerusalem was the captured Al Aqsa Mosque on Temple Mount, which was believed to be the ancient site of King Solomon's temple, it was later rumoured that the Templars may have unearthed long-forgotten secrets of Solomon, or the Hebrew Ark of the Covenant or the sacred chalice of Christ-Jesus' Passover meal.

Moreover, the lurid accounts of Templar knights worshipping a heathen idol called "Baphomet" (a mistranslation of "Mahomet" = Muhammad), or engaging in acts of sexual depravity, or conducting ceremonial blasphemy against the crucifix were entirely fallacious information obtained from knights under horrific duress by King Philip IV of France. The sinister king of France was heavily indebted to the Templar Order to help finance a protracted war for control of the English monarchy; so to avoid repayment and to seize their communal wealth, Philip arrested, tortured and executed innocent Templar knights, including the grand master of the order, Jacques de Molay. Philip also falsely arrested and expelled Jewish citizens from French territories in order to seize their assets as well.

When King Philip began to levy unfair taxes against the French clergy in order to continue financing his costly war, he was soundly condemned by Pope Boniface VIII. Whereupon, Philip abducted the pope by surprise retaliation in Italy and installed his own puppet pope, Clement V, in Poitiers, France. Under pressure from King Philip, Pope Clement ordered all Christian monarchs in Europe to arrest the Templars and to seize their assets. Further military threats by Philip forced Clement to officially dissolve the order in 1312 and to turn over most of their remaining assets to the Knights of St. John (also known as the Knights of Malta or the Knights Hospitallers).

While some Templars certainly found safe haven in Scotland and Switzerland, which were outside the sphere of papal influence at this time since both territories had been previously excommunicated, many knights simply joined other orders, particularly the equally powerful Order of St. John. The Templar Order in Portugal continued to survive with the assistance of King Denis by simply changing its name and re-instituting as the Military Order of Christ. Some Templars in other countries were arrested and tried, but never convicted. Some knights were even pensioned off and left to retire peacefully. Remarkably, a misplaced document was found in the Vatican Secret Archives in 2002 that records the trial of the Templars and the fact that before dissolving the order in 1312 Pope Clement in 1308 actually absolved the accused Templars of all heresies against them. Unfortunately, that did not prevent the corrupt Philip IV from burning alive at the stake Grand Master de Molay and Normandy Master de Charney in Paris on March 19, 1314.

4.8   Templars and Freemasonry

So any modern-day orders, particularly Masonic, claiming to have a Templar connection are clearly spurious. The Templars were a Catholic monastic order established in the Middle Ages to provide military protection for Christian pilgrims to the Holy Lands. This once-essential service is no longer required, and since the Order has been officially dissolved in its original form by the Church, there are no recognized Templar knights remaining today. Without official Catholic approval, any group or individual claiming to be Templar is simply bogus. Moreover, it would be interesting to know if any of these Masonic would-be Templars take strict monastic vows of poverty, chastity, piety and obedience; or faithfully abide by the 72 instructions of the Latin Rule.

Though some Masonic legends claim that Freemasonry was actually started by exiled Templars or that persecuted Templars took safety within certain Masonic orders (in Scotland, for example), such conjecture makes no logical sense whatsoever. Firstly, feudal brotherhoods of stonemasons were in existence long before the Order of Templars was endorsed by the Church in 1129; so the

Templars certainly didn't establish Freemasonry. Secondly, while it is possible that desperate Templars could have temporarily hidden out in the guarded lodges of stonemasons, it is more likely that as Christian warrior-monks they would have sought refuge in any number of sympathetic monastic orders in Europe at the time.

The idea, however, that there was close contact between Templars and stonemasons is certainly logical. Since the Templars established a network of stone temples, castles and fortifications stretching from Britain to Jerusalem, they obviously would have employed an army of talented stonemasons to do the necessary construction. But since one was a military monastic order and the other was a practicing guild of tradesmen, their only commonality was their Christian faith and loyalty to the Holy Church.

The only reason that de-Christianized Freemasonry includes degrees and orders of pseudo-Templarism is the mistaken mystique that the Templars were not dedicated and devout Christian military monks but deceitful purveyors and practitioners of ancient pagan mysteries. Since modern Freemasonry cloaks itself in secrecy and deceit, it quite naturally looks for these qualities in other brotherhoods.

4.9   Templars and the Holy Grail

The truth is that the Templars did uncover and safeguard certain sacred treasures that had been acquired in the Middle East; but these were sacred relics associated with Christianity, not fragments of old pagan mystery knowledge. The Templars were documented to have possessed a piece of the true wooden cross of Christ. Also, the mummified head that the Templars were falsely accused of worshipping was actually a relic that the Order was known to possess, the head of St. Euphemia of Chalcedon. Also, the recorded "confessions" of the tortured knights in Paris makes mention of the Order possessing a red, monochromatic, full-length image of a man on linen or cotton cloth. This was clearly a reference to the famous Shroud of Turin, since the first known public display of the shroud in 1357 was by the family of the grandson of Geoffrey de Charney, the unfortunate Templar who was burned at the stake with Grand Master de Molay in 1314.

On a much deeper esoteric level, the Templars did indeed unknowingly stumble across an essential aspect of the mystery of the Holy Grail. Through their intense devotion and enthusiastic fervour as faithful servants of Christ-Jesus, Templar knights were to passionately feel that their entire lives had been turned over to the Risen Saviour. When they thought, it was Christ-Jesus thinking in them; when they felt, it was Christ-Jesus feeling in them; when they acted, it was Christ-Jesus acting through them. Every breath they took was intimately felt to be Christ-Jesus breathing in them; the beating of their heart and the coursing of blood through their veins was experienced as the life of Christ-Jesus in their bodies. As described by Rudolf Steiner in a lecture on 2 October 1916:

> The blood of the Templars belonged to Christ Jesus—each one of them knew this. Their blood belonged to nothing else on earth than to Christ Jesus. Every moment of their life was to be filled with the perpetual consciousness of how in their own soul there dwelt—in the words of St. Paul—'not I, but Christ in me'! And in bloody and severe combat, in devoted work such as the Crusades demanded, the Templars put into practice what they had spiritually undertaken to do … to establish more firmly in earth existence the impulse which came from the Mystery of Golgotha. (Published in *The Knights Templar: The Mystery of the Warrior Monks*; 2011)

By mystically uniting their own blood with the spiritualized blood of the resurrected Saviour in the etheric sphere of the earth, the Knights Templar inadvertently experienced a form of Christian initiation whereby they contacted the real presence of Christ-Jesus in the supernatural realm. By uniquely experiencing the "sangréal" (Spanish for 'royal blood') of Christ—the "san gréal" or 'Holy Grail'—the Templar initiates actually reflected the egohood of Christ-Jesus in their souls; thereby releasing true supernatural light into the world. Once again, as described by Rudolf Steiner:

> Something quite remarkable and powerful had thus entered into the circle of the Templar Order without their having known the rules of Christian initiation other than through sacrificial service ... This experience of the Templars meant that the Mystery of Golgotha was understood, and also experienced, at a higher stage than before. Something was now present in the world with regard to the Mystery of Golgotha which was previously not there ... These external deeds and the enthusiasm that lived in these deeds drew out the souls of the Templars so that these souls, being separated from the body, outside the body, lived with the spiritual progress of humanity and penetrated in soul and spirit the secrets of the Mystery of Golgotha. They then underwent many and deep experiences, and not for the individual soul alone but for all humanity. (Ibid)

Tragically, however, in spite of its grandeur and sublimity, the unintentional and spontaneously generated initiation of the Templars caused them to become anomalies in progressive human development. Their accelerated esoteric advancement placed them outside the stream of exoteric Christianity to which they properly belonged; but their connection to the medieval Roman Catholic Church excluded them from the normal stream of esoteric Christianity as well.

The Templars, then, became a religious order without a spiritual home. Moreover, since their abnormally rapid attainment prematurely expanded their consciousness beyond the safe confines of the body, the Templars also unknowingly opened themselves to Luciferic assault. Due to his diabolic lust for gold and power, Philip IV became the eager agent of Luciferic powers who sought to destroy the Templars and thereby halt the influx of Christ-light that was pouring into the world through them.

Thankfully, in the great hall of cosmic justice, the cruelly-murdered Templar knights found fair and lawful recompense. Their premature deaths flooded the supernatural world closest to the earth with radiant Christ-light that illumined and inspired the Christian souls descending to birth into Renaissance Europe. Many an enlightened intellect during that period could trace the source of their brilliance to Jacques de Molay and to the Christ-filled Templars on the other side of the veil.

CHAPTER 5

THE ROSICRUCIAN MYSTERIES:
LAZARUS COMES FORTH AGAIN

5.1   Rosicrucian Secrecy

NO OTHER HIDDEN brotherhood has enflamed the inner aspirations and evoked the ardent imaginations of countless seekers of esoteric illumination down through the post-Renaissance centuries more than the illustrious Order of the Rose-Cross, the mysterious Fraternity of Rosicrucians. And yet, prior to the detailed information publicly revealed for the first time by Rudolf Steiner, almost nothing was reliably known about them.

What we know from Steiner's supersensible research is that the authentic Rosicrucian Order is not a fictitious historical fabrication; but that, amazingly, this mysterious brotherhood of esoteric Christian initiates has been in hidden existence as far back as the thirteenth century. So why this great cloak of invisibility; and does this mean that the Rosicrucians have been detached and aloof from the world, choosing to remain insular, self-absorbed and inactive?

Actually, nothing could be further from the truth. Many a new scientific discovery, technological invention, work of art, literary publication, theological insight, philanthropic endeavour or social improvement can be traced back to an inconspicuous Rosicrucian inspiration. Rosicrucian initiates have historically preferred to remain anonymous, inspiring others to do their important work in the world.

Such a necessary course of action is certainly not because of an exclusionist desire to jealously guard esoteric secrets for their own personal possession (as is done in Freemasonry) or because they are engaged in politically nefarious or subversive activity (as is done in "brotherhoods of the left"). As sincere Christian esotericists, Rosicrucian initiates are well aware that restricted sectarian access to supernatural knowledge and experience is contrary to the intentions of Christ-Jesus, who came to reveal the mysteries of God, to open up the "secrets kept hidden since the foundation of the world." Moreover, Christ-Jesus has made these mysteries available to all mankind, to "whosoever will," if they sincerely knock on the door to the inner temple of wisdom—the sanctuary of the Holy Spirit.

The portal of entry to the School of the Rose-Cross, therefore, has always been freely open to sincere Christian aspirants who have properly prepared their inner lives to serve the mission of Christ-Jesus. Likewise, it has always remained hidden from the eyes of the merely curious, the selfish seekers, the unprepared and those who seek to do harm. Surprising as it may seem to the sensitive at heart, there are powerful individuals, groups, supernatural beings and forces in existence that are vehemently opposed to the influx of divine light and love into our world, and who actually prefer to remain in spiritual darkness and in egotistic, God-separated isolation.

A further reason for the continuing policy of strict anonymity of Rosicrucian teachers and students is to avoid undue veneration by others. Through accelerated development, Rosicrucian initiates have acquired supernatural knowledge and abilities that ordinary humanity will only unfold in the far distant future. As potent centres of Christ-light, there is always the danger that the Rosicrucian initiate becomes an unhealthy focus of extreme adulation and excessive hero-worship by impressionable followers. Likewise, if true Rosicrucians are publicly known then they also become sure targets of constant and concerted psychic attack from enemies of the light. The extreme reactions that inevitably follow from being in the social spotlight, therefore, would usually hinder or prevent the good work that the Rosicrucian initiate is attempting to achieve.[20]

In spite of the psychic risks involved, a recent and notable exception to the usual practice of protective anonymity was made by Rosicrucian initiate, Rudolf Steiner. As a well-known public figure, Steiner directly and openly revealed a wealth of Rosicrucian history, theology, training methodology and developmental practices that had previously been silently safeguarded strictly within the confines of the brotherhood. Though Steiner was able to effectively deal with the risk of undesirable emulation, he was certainly under constant psychic attack throughout his public career. Fortunately for progressive human development, this physical and supernatural assault did not overly hinder his vitally important work in the world.

5.2   Christian Rosenkreutz: The Founder of the Order

One of Steiner's important pronouncements in the area of Rosicrucian history was to confirm the actual historical existence of Christian Rosenkreutz as the true founder of the Rosicrucian brotherhood. Moreover, since Rosicrucianism is a modern-day form of esoteric Christianity, it is perhaps no surprise that the figure of Christian Rosenkreutz was a later incarnation of St. John the Beloved, the disciple designated by Christ-Jesus to institute the stream of esoteric Christianity.

Here again, as with Christ-Jesus himself, it is important to be clear that Brother CRC (as he was referred to in Rosicrucian circles) did not attempt to resurrect the ancient pagan mysteries; that is, to re-establish a modern-day Mystery school in imitation of the old Mysteries. What he did do was to establish an esoteric school of Christianity that was suited to the demands of the modern, intellectual, scientific age; an advanced school in which to comprehend, to teach and to embody the new, greater mysteries of Christ-Jesus. As the Messiah was the fulfillment of all the elevating exoteric and esoteric religious impulses of the ancient past, so similarly—as a profound disciple of our Saviour—Christian Rosenkreutz synthesized and Christianized within his own soul the twelve major religious streams from Atlantean times to the late Middle Ages. As a result of this special initiatory process, Christian Rosenkreutz was able to further reflect the divine life of Christ-Jesus within himself—to mystically incorporate the redeemed ego-soul of Christ-Jesus—and on this basis to pattern the Rosicrucian Order as a human-initiated reflection of Christ-Jesus and the twelve apostles.

As with the Messiah's dual ordering of discipleship, within the Rosicrucian Order there is an inner circle of twelve and an outer circle of many. The original twelve disciples, who came together in the thirteenth-century, were composed of seven highly-advanced individuals who had previously been the seven holy Rishis in prehistoric India and whose souls had faithfully preserved the oracle-wisdom from old Atlantis. Four other disciples each incorporated a distillate of knowledge from one of the four post-Atlantean cultural periods: the ancient Indian, the ancient Persian, the Egypto-Chaldean and the Graeco-Roman. The last disciple represented the future, fifth post-Atlantean cultural period, the European, which didn't begin until the birth of the Renaissance in the fifteenth century. From century to century, each of the twelve was required to find a suitable replacement before their demise. That way, the inner circle of twelve was perpetually maintained, even by later embodiments of the original twelve. The central, thirteenth member of the circle of twelve was of course Christian Rosenkreutz (St. John), since he stands as the emissary of Christ-Jesus within the stream of esoteric Christianity.

The outer circle of the Rosicrucian Order is comprised mainly of esoteric pupils who have been supernaturally chosen by Christian Rosenkreutz himself. These initiates are from all walks of life and in all parts of the earth. This circle is not required to gather together geographically but is karmically joined to Christian Rosenkreutz and given instruction and assistance telepathically, though on rare occasions this has been done through physical appearance as well.

Since Christian Rosenkreutz, or Master John (as he is also known), is one of the twelve bodhisattvas, the Rosicrucian brotherhood is supernaturally connected to the great lodge of humanity. As such, although Master John is the central teacher of the Rosicrucian stream, other bodhisattvas are also involved as illustrious teachers of the Order; such as Manes (Manu), Zarathas (Zarathustra), Boddha (Gautama Buddha), Scythianos (Serapis) and in the twentieth century, Master Thomas (Rudolf Steiner).[21]

Concerning Christian Rosenkreutz in his biblical incarnation as St. John, we learn from Rosicrucian teaching that John the Evangelist is not the same individual as John the Apostle, the son of Zebedee and brother of James the Greater. Even modern scholarship makes a distinction between "John the Apostle," one of the original disciples, and "John the Evangelist," the presumed author of The Gospel According to John, as being two distinct individuals. In

Rosicrucianism, Christian Rosenkreutz, as John the Evangelist (not John the Apostle), did indeed write the gospel attributed to him as well as The Apocalypse (The Revelation to John).

What is unusual about The Gospel According to John is that nowhere in the writing is the name "John" ever mentioned, only "the disciple whom Jesus loved." For example, at the last supper: "One of his disciples, whom Jesus loved, was lying close to the breast of Jesus" (John 13:23); at the foot of the cross: "When Jesus saw his mother, and the disciple whom he loved" (John 19:26); on the day of resurrection: "So she [Mary Magdalene] ran, and went to Simon Peter and the other disciple, the one whom Jesus loved" (John 20:2); when Jesus appeared by the lake in resurrected form: "That disciple whom Jesus loved said to Peter, 'It is the Lord!'" (John 21:7); and when Christ was giving instructions regarding the establishment of the new Christian faith: "Peter turned and saw following them the disciple whom Jesus loved, who had lain close to his breast at the supper" (John 21:20).

The only other instances in John's gospel where a similar phrase is used is in reference to Lazarus, who Christ-Jesus raised from the dead, as in the following: "Lord, he [Lazarus] whom you love is ill" (John 11:3); and "So the Jews said, 'See how he loved him [Lazarus]' (John 11:36). From these passages, then, we see evidence of the Rosicrucian teaching that John the Evangelist and the disciple Lazarus are one and the same individual—the individual who later reincarnated as Christian Rosenkreutz. It is further understood that raising Lazarus from the dead was actually an initiatory event in which Lazarus was carefully placed in a death-like condition for three-and-a-half days and then later revived by Christ-Jesus acting as the hierophant-initiator. The purposely-induced cataleptic state necessary for Lazarus' initiation explains the puzzling words of Christ-Jesus as recorded in scripture:

> But when Jesus heard [that Lazarus was deathly ill] he said, 'This illness is not unto death; it is for the glory of God, so that the Son of God may be glorified by means of it … Our friend Lazarus has fallen asleep, but I go to awake him out of sleep." (John 11:4, 11)

What this initiatory event signified was that, prior to his own death and resurrection, the incarnated Christ-Jesus still needed to use the "temple trance" procedure of the ancient Mysteries in order to consciously connect Lazarus to his radiant sun-nature in the supernatural realm. What is hugely important to note, however, was that the initiation of Lazarus did not take place within the secret confines of a Mystery temple, but in full public view—out in the open for all to observe. This event, then, was a necessary transition from the old, secret, exclusionist pagan Mysteries to the new, open, accessible Christian mysteries that would be fully established by Christ-Jesus through his death, resurrection and ascension.

Since consciously experiencing the supernatural realm fundamentally transformed the initiate, he felt as though reborn; he was a new person, a "dweller in two worlds." As such, it was customary to adopt a new initiatory name; in the case of Lazarus, he became "John." A similar custom is also retained in the Catholic Church when candidates for the Sacrament of Confirmation choose the name of a saint as their new initiatory name. Moreover, the phrase "the disciple whom Jesus loved" is esoterically understood to mean the disciple who was personally initiated by Christ-Jesus. This understanding is also reflected in the name "John the Beloved."

Once Christ-Jesus had transformed and resurrected fallen human nature through his death on the cross and thereby reopened the gates of heaven; that is, re-established conscious access to the supernatural realm, then initiation became entirely possible through the new Christ-forces infused within every human soul. Even though Lazarus/John had been personally initiated by Christ-Jesus prior to the crucifixion, it was still the old trance method that soon became ineffectual. Consequently, in the thirteenth century Christian Rosenkreutz still needed to undergo the new Christian initiation whereby the Risen Saviour is personally encountered in full consciousness within the supernatural aura of the earth. Moreover, this process needed to be accomplished completely without exterior trance inducement and without external hierophant assistance and control, but entirely through the Christ-infused forces of his own soul. Only by fully experiencing the new Christian initiation himself could Christian Rosenkreutz establish a suitable esoteric path for other seekers materialistically immersed in the unfurling Age of Reason—the path of Rosicrucian-Christianity.

5.3   Rosicrucian Publications

Since the true Rosicrucian Order (even to the present day) has never been publicly accessible, the dozens and dozens of Rosicrucian organizations that have wildly sprung up since the seventeenth-century, each claiming to be authentic, are all entirely bogus. Some pseudo-Rosicrucian societies may indeed possess fragments of Rosicrucian wisdom that have been partially released to the public since the seventeenth and eighteenth centuries, but this information certainly does not originate with them. In accordance with the protective practices of the Order, early Rosicrucian releases were done anonymously, though in some instances authorship could be traced back to specific individuals who acted (sometimes unknowingly) under Rosicrucian inspiration.

One example of this is the *Secret Symbols of the Rosicrucians of the 16th and 17th Centuries* (in three volumes) released in

1785–1788 by "A Brother of the Fraternity." The anonymous authorship was later attributed to Hinricus Madathanus Theosophus, a pseudonym of German physician and alchemist, Adrian von Mynsicht (1603–1638). Other earlier examples are the *Fama Fraternitatis Rosae Crucis* (*The Fame of the Brotherhood of the Rose Cross*, 1614); the *Confessio Fraternitatis* (*The Confession of the Society and Brotherhood of the Rose Cross*, 1615); and the *Chymical Wedding of Christian Rosenkreutz in the Year 1459*, (1616). The anonymous authorship of these three works has been attributed to the German theologian, Johann Valentin Andreae (1586–1654).

5.4 Rosicrucianism and Freemasonry

Speculative Freemasonry has also vainly attempted to connect itself to Rosicrucianism by offering a Knight of the Rose Cross Degree (18°) in the appended system commonly referred to as the "Scottish Rite." It has been suggested that this degree is a token attempt by Freemasonry to include some element of Christianity into its otherwise lukewarm deist beliefs. However, since Masonic initiates are free to interpret any specific Christian symbols, allegories and references according to their personal religious background, the Rose Cross degree isn't necessarily Christian.

As with modern Freemasonry's equally contradictory attempt to connect with the Catholic Order of Knights Templar, the true Fraternity of the Rose-Cross has little in common with a deliberately de-Christianized secret society such as Freemasonry. The Rosicrucians are an esoteric Christian brotherhood devoutly interested in properly unveiling the greater mysteries of Christ-Jesus; not in preserving and regenerating the old pagan mysteries. Sadly, even today Freemasonic literature still states that the order is "Erected to God and dedicated to the Holy Saints John [the

Evangelist and the Baptist]." This is clearly a forgotten reminder of when Freemasonry was a medieval guild of Christian workmen, at a time when each working association in Christendom had its specific patron saint.

This indicates the real tragedy of modern, de-Christianized Freemasonry: in the early Christian centuries, it too was inspired, nurtured and cultivated by the individuality of St. John the Beloved. No doubt many of today's Freemasons, who have been deliberately kept ill-informed by their hidden superiors, would be surprised to know the Rosicrucian truth that Hiram Abiff, the illustrious master-builder of their Temple Legend, was an earlier incarnation of St. John the Beloved. By anachronistically focusing their entire mythology on Hiram Abiff, speculative Freemasonry has not esoterically advanced together with the master-builder of the fraternity in his later incarnations as St. John and as Christian Rosenkreutz.

Regrettably, as a result modern Freemasonry has now become the shadow side of true Rosicrucianism: the Order of Freemasons currently stands as the esoteric antithesis of the Order of the Rose-Cross. Where Rosicrucianism looks to Christ-Jesus and to the future, Freemasonry looks to Lucifer and to the past. Where Rosicrucianism seeks to unveil and to share the new Christian mysteries, Freemasonry seeks to conceal and to hoard the old Luciferic mysteries.

CHAPTER 6

THEOSOPHY AND BLAVATSKY: LUCIFERIC MYSTERIES IN VICTORIAN ATTIRE

6.1 The Rosicrucian Roots of Theosophy

AS WELL AS Freemasonry, a more recent, spectacular esoteric initiative of Master John that was systematically hijacked by Luciferic forces was Theosophy. According to Rudolf Steiner, the original founding of the Theosophical Movement and Society in 1875 by Helena Blavatsky (1831–1891), Henry Olcott (1832–1907) and William Judge (1851–1896) was under the dual Rosicrucian inspiration and sponsorship of Master John and Master Zarathas.[22]

The central Rosicrucian intention in this instance was to establish a worldwide movement together with a public society as a modern means of openly promulgating esoteric (theosophical) Christian knowledge. As such, the Theosophical Movement would be an entirely new phenomenon in world history—a universally accessible esoteric movement (not a religion) linked to the supernatural realm through the Rosicrucian Order. Likewise, the accompanying Theosophical Society would be a completely new institution in world history—a legally registered public society also esoterically linked to the supernatural realm through the Rosicrucian Order. The promulgation of esoteric knowledge would be in a clear, intellectual format consistent with modern thinking, and made accessible to the general public through modern media (such as books, lectures, journals and lessons).

The vital mission of the Theosophical Movement and Society was to counteract the oppressive materialistic worldview of the mid-nineteenth century that was threatening to dominate human thinking in the very near future. The viral spread of a radical materialism that completely denied any supernatural component to reality would be severely destructive to progressive human development.

This impending crisis in the spiritual life of humanity also alarmed a number of secret brotherhoods in Europe, America and Asia that were far less enlightened than the Rosicrucian Order. Their collective solution (after much disagreement) was to introduce in the early nineteenth century a religious movement in the West, termed "Spiritualism" in America and "Spiritism" in Europe. Since these secret brotherhoods were all atavistic organizations preserving the old, pre-Christian mysteries, their only means of contacting the supernatural realm was through anachronistic "mediumship." This was an occult practice previously used only within the closed confines of these dubious brotherhoods; whereby, a particularly sensitive individual (the "medium") was placed in a deep, trance-like condition for a short period of time in order to establish an unconscious contact with the supernatural realm. Paranormal information could then be verbally elicited from the tranced medium.

Trance mediumship was, of course, a deteriorated form of the old temple sleep that was once practiced in the ancient

Mysteries. As a possible solution to radical materialism, the Spiritualist/Spiritist movement introduced trance mediumship to the general public. Mediumistic communications with supernatural entities usually took the form of group séances; that is, small gatherings held in dimly-lit private salons. At first, the movement attracted wide and serious attention, but very quickly degenerated into a fraudulent, sub-astral and psychically-damaging enterprise. Hoards of phony mediums intent on scamming money from credulous participants quickly invaded the movement. Likewise, authentic mediums quickly became astrally invaded by discarnate entities and reprobate souls in the after-death realm who were more intent on psychic mischief than on conveying truthful information about the supernatural realm.

Trance mediumship was never a method of acquiring Rosicrucian wisdom. The Rosicrucian-Christian path of initiation has always demanded full conscious awareness, stringent intellectual clarity and virtuous moral adherence. For these reasons, Master John had no part in the Spiritualist Movement. Unfortunately, prior to the latter half of the nineteenth century it was exceedingly difficult to present esoteric information in clear conceptual form. Since the thirteenth century, natural and supernatural conditions had necessitated that esoteric truths be conveyed mostly in symbolic picture forms, referred to in Rosicrucian teaching as "Imaginations." It was therefore difficult to find a suitably developed initiate *outside* the Rosicrucian fraternity through which crucially-needed, esoteric wisdom could intellectually flow into the materialistic culture of the time.

6.2   Helena Petrovna Blavatsky

A remarkable individual did capture the clairvoyant attention of Master John as a suitable transition figure to prepare the social and intellectual climate that would enable a more complete Rosicrucian outpouring at the end of the nineteenth century. That individual was, of course, Helena Petrovna Blavatsky. Madame Blavatsky, or HPB as she was affectionately called, possessed a curious range of natural psychic gifts. For one, she was a highly-developed trance medium who was able to provide far more comprehensive supernatural information than all others at the time. Even more exceptionally, Madame Blavatsky was able to later recall the information that she conveyed while in a deep, somnolent trance. She was also able to consciously soul-travel when out of the body during sleep, and to be in telepathic rapport with advanced initiates while still awake.

Through her extraordinary talents as a medium, HPB was involved for a time in the Spiritualist Movement in America, from where she met Henry Olcott, William Judge and the others who together would later establish Theosophy. Her mediumship gifts, no matter how exceptional, were of little interest to Rosicrucian Master John. Her acute telepathic skills, however, permitted a torrent of hidden or forgotten esoteric literature to be transmitted through her and to be copied down in a readable format. In this way, Master John was able to provide much of the early esoteric material in Blavatsky's first Theosophical publication in two volumes entitled, *Isis Unveiled* (1877).[23]

HPB's ability to lucidly soul-travel also enabled her to receive inner-plane instruction from Master John and Master Zarathas concerning the establishment of the Theosophical Movement and the Society. In this way, the customary, protective anonymity of the Rosicrucian masters would be maintained. Nevertheless, in the early years of Theosophy, Master John also met physically with HPB on several occasions to elicit her assistance and to provide valuable advice.

Physical contact was possible since Master John had been

in continual embodiment since his incarnation in the late seventeenth century as the son of Prince Francis II of the Hungarian House of Rákóczy. In adulthood, Master John was later known throughout European society by the title of the Count of Saint-Germain. Consequently, to early Theosophists such as HPB he was not referred to as Master John or Christian Rosenkreutz but was better known as "The Count," or as "Master Rákóczy" or simply as "Master R." The unusual longevity of this Rosicrucian master was of course due to the remarkable powers of regeneration that he had acquired in becoming an advanced bodhisattva.

Unfortunately, but not surprisingly, HPB had also attracted the partisan attention of various secret brotherhoods in America, Europe and Asia that wanted to use her remarkable mediumistic abilities for their own hidden, political agendas. Since Rosicrucian Master John, in devout conformity to Christ-Jesus, never exerts coercive control or undue influencing over his pupils, HPB was always free to pursue whatever course of action she decided. Regrettably, she decided to become involved with some of these disreputable brotherhoods.

Since these brotherhoods jealously hoard their esoteric secrets for their own selfish purposes, any independent attempt by Blavatsky to publicize knowledge she acquired from them was fiercely forbidden. To maintain psychic control over Blavatsky, fearful Western initiates occultly enclosed her in dark astral forces, thereby incapacitating her powers of psychic memory: her ability to recall prior esoteric knowledge within her soul. In this way, their secrets were safe, but Blavatsky now fell under increased occult manipulation by shadowy initiates.

Since this lamentable situation was the predictable outcome of Blavatsky's free exercise of poor judgement, her erratic and volatile personality and her unreasonable demands and ambitions, she could no longer serve as a reliable outlet for the esoteric Rosicrucian wisdom issuing from the bodhisattvas of the West: Master John and Master Zarathas.

Soon after the publication of *Isis Unveiled* in 1877, Blavatsky was freed from her psychic confinement by shadowy Eastern initiates (primarily from India) who had covertly arranged with the Western brotherhoods to keep Blavatsky quiet regarding Western secrets by moving her and the Society headquarters to India. Since Blavatsky was born and raised in the Ukraine and had studied in Tibet for two years while travelling in her youth, her extraordinary psychic gifts had already attracted the attention of the authentic bodhisattvas of the East, Master Morya and Master Kuthumi. For many years they had acted as her spiritual mentors and guides.

So when Blavatsky and Olcott moved to India in 1879 and later established the Society's international headquarters in Adyar in 1882, she mistakenly thought this activity was under the direction of Master M and Master KH. What Blavatsky didn't know was that inferior Indian initiates "of the left-hand path" were fraudulently impersonating the Eastern bodhisattvas (the "mahatmas") in order to furtively use her for their own religious and political agenda. It was their intention to use Blavatsky and Theosophy to ignite a religious revival of Buddhism and Hinduism in the East, then to flood the West with Eastern esotericism and, most importantly, to politically expel the British and the Western brotherhoods from colonial India.

In effect, then, Blavatsky and Theosophy were diverted from their original, Western-oriented Rosicrucian direction and occultly kidnapped to the East. In accordance with cosmic law, the march of human progress and civilization in post-Atlantean times has proceeded from east to west—from ancient India; to ancient Persia; to ancient Egypt and Chaldea; to ancient Greece and Rome; then to modern Europe, Russia and America. To move the Rosicrucian-inspired, Theosophical Movement and Society to the East was to proceed in a backward, retrograde direction. However justified the religious and nationalistic aspirations of the Eastern initiates, the glaring and sweeping result was that Theosophy became regressive rather than progressive and Luciferic rather than Christocentric.

6.3   Theosophy and Lucifer

Theosophically rejecting Christ-Jesus and embracing Lucifer was made all the easier with Blavatsky's open and fervent hostility toward Judaism and Christianity. As described by Rudolf Steiner:

> In considering Blavatsky, it is important that her attitude was what might well be called anti-Christian … It becomes abundantly clear that she had a deep sympathy for all religions in the world except Judaism and Christianity, and that she had a deep antipathy toward Judaism and Christianity. Blavatsky depicts everything deriving from the latter as inferior to the great revelations of the various pagan religions: in other words, she manifests an expressly anti-Christian perspective, but an expressly spiritual one. (From a lecture given on 13 June 1923 and published in *Spiritualism, Madam Blavatsky, and Theosophy*; 2002)

Blavatsky didn't even regard Christ-Jesus as an actual historical figure, but rather as a totally fabricated myth. This anti-Christian prejudice had even crept into the earlier, Rosicrucian-inspired *Isis Unveiled*, as indicated by the following:

> The present volumes have been written to small purpose if they have not shown, 1, that Jesus, the Christ-God, is a myth concocted two centuries after the real Hebrew Jesus died; 2, that, therefore, he never had any authority to give

Peter, or anyone else, plenary power; 3, that, even if he had given such authority, the word Petra (rock) referred to the revealed truths of the Petroma, not to him who thrice denied him; and that besides, the apostolic succession is a gross and palpable fraud; 4, that the *Gospel according to Matthew* is a fabrication based on a wholly different manuscript. The whole thing, therefore, is an imposition alike upon priest and penitent.

Once Blavatsky and company decided to headquarter in India, then Theosophy became the public face of fraudulent Eastern mahatmas who were intent on strengthening the occult power of the East over the culture and secret brotherhoods of the West. The Western brotherhoods, however, were not about to have their occult power and control usurped.

In 1885, the British Psychical Research Society issued an investigative report concluding that Blavatsky was a fraud. Much of this evidence was based on "Mahatma Letters," correspondence alleged to have miraculously appeared from the Eastern masters, but which were claimed to be surreptitiously delivered by Mme. Coulomb, an assistant to Blavatsky. This information was obtained from some "Protestant missionaries" in Madras at the time. According to the PRS report:

> [Blavatsky was] neither the mouthpiece of hidden seers, nor ... a mere vulgar adventuress; we think she has achieved title to permanent remembrance as one of the most accomplished, ingenious and interesting imposters in history.

Clearly this was a designed attack by the Western brotherhoods to discredit Blavatsky and Theosophy in order to bury any esoteric secrets that she might reveal in the future under a stifling layer of controversy.[24]

Predictably, the scandal had a demoralizing effect on

Blavatsky which in turn exacerbated her chronic ill-health. This forced her in 1885 to leave India and move to Italy; then to Wurzburg, Germany and finally to London, England. Remarkably, despite her compromised health, Blavatsky was able to publish her second major opus in two volumes, *The Secret Doctrine*, in 1888. This work, written under the inspiration of the Indian mahatmas, was a strange syncretistic brew of Gnostic notions, Neoplatonic philosophy, pagan mystery wisdom, Buddhism, Hinduism and Western mysticism. Moreover, it further alarmed the Western brotherhoods with the continued betrayal of their own jealously-guarded secrets and with the astonishing esoteric knowledge it contained that was entirely unknown to them. Fortunately for these brotherhoods, or perhaps because of their renewed psychic assault, Blavatsky fatally succumbed to Bright's disease and influenza three years later in 1891.

The Secret Doctrine was clearly bathed in a Luciferic light. It regurgitated the Gnostic notion that Lucifer, the serpent in paradise, was the true benefactor of humanity; and that the demiurgic creator-god, Yahweh, was the enemy of human progress. Blavatsky stated this position clearly and unabashedly in Volume II, entitled "Anthropogenesis," where she equated Lucifer and Satan in the following way:

> Satan will now be shown, in the teaching of the Secret Doctrine, allegorized as Good, and Sacrifice, a God of Wisdom, under different names ... In this case it is but natural—even from the dead letter standpoint—to view *Satan*, the Serpent of Genesis, as the real creator and benefactor, the Father of Spiritual mankind. For it is he who was the "Harbinger of Light," bright radiant Lucifer, who opened the eyes of the automaton *created* by Jehovah, as alleged; and he who was the first to whisper: "in the day ye eat thereof ye shall be as Elohim, knowing good and evil"—can only be regarded in the light of a Saviour. An "adversary" to Jehovah the "*personating* spirit," he still

remains in esoteric truth the ever-loving "Messenger" (the Angel), the Seraphim and Cherubim who both *knew* well, and *loved* still more, and who conferred on us spiritual, instead of physical immortality—the latter a kind of *static* immortality that would have transformed man into an undying "Wandering Jew."

After Blavatsky left India and continuing after her death, Henry Olcott as president of the Theosophical Society extensively travelled throughout India, Ceylon, Japan, Australia, Europe and the United States strengthening the administrative arm of Theosophy. Under Olcott's capable leadership, the Society continued to vigorously grow and expand until his own death in 1907; whereupon he was succeeded as president by social reformer turned theosophist, Annie Besant (1847–1933). Even though Besant continued the Eastern, anti-Christian, Luciferic orientation of the International Society and willingly submitted to the control of clandestine Indian mahatmas, the Rosicrucian masters made one last concerted attempt to turn Theosophy around to its original Christocentric purpose.

CHAPTER 7

ANTHROPOSOPHY: OPENING ALL MYSTERIES TO THE LIGHT OF DAY

7.1   Rudolf Steiner and Theosophy

IN 1902, ROSICRUCIAN initiate Rudolf Steiner became the head of the German Section of the Theosophical Society. Initially with Besant's agreement and acceptance, Steiner faithfully pursued an independent Western approach to esoteric (theosophical) knowledge based on his own clairvoyant research, not on tradition or on mediumistic results. This Western focus also included the esoteric study of Christianity and natural science.

While membership in the German Section of the Theosophical Society rapidly grew under Steiner's influence and leadership (from a few individuals in a single lodge to sixty-nine lodges by 1913), the rest of the Theosophical Society remained firmly rooted in Eastern esotericism Instead of returning Theosophy to its original Rosicrucian purpose, Steiner's resplendent outpouring of Western

Christocentric esotericism soon resulted in an ideological polarization of the membership along Eastern and Western lines.

Besant had been instructed by Blavatsky before her death that once Theosophy had become firmly established in the world, its primary mission was to prepare mankind for the imminent return of "Christ in the twentieth century." But since Theosophy had become anti-Christian and Easternized, the true person of Christ-Jesus and the true nature of his return were completely misunderstood.

Theosophy under Besant's leadership believed that the real historical Jesus was born about 150 BC and was called (according to some Talmudic writings) Yeshua ben Pandira—Jesus, son of Pandira. This earlier Jesus was believed to have been overshadowed by the Bodhisattva Maitreya, who used him as a physical means of expression.[25] The return of Christ in the twentieth century, therefore, was envisioned by Besant and other Theosophists, particularly Charles W. Leadbeater (1854–1934), to be a similar occurrence. A suitable male child would be chosen and esoterically trained to be the bearer of "Maitreya the Christ," who would then usher in a new age of enlightenment. In 1909, Leadbeater announced that he had found the perfect vessel, a young Indian boy named Jiddu Krishnamurti (1895–1986). A new organization, the Order of the Star in the East (OSE), was established in 1911 to prepare the world for the "Coming of the World Teacher."

To Rosicrucian initiate Rudolf Steiner, what was being taught and promoted by the Theosophical Society under Annie Besant as the "Coming of Christ" was a horrible distortion of the esoteric truth. Though it was true that the Bodhisattva Maitreya had indwelt the bodily vehicles of Jesus the son of Pandira more than a century BC, he was not the historical Christ-Jesus; but is instead the future successor to Gautama Buddha. Even more importantly, according to

Rosicrucian teaching and Steiner's own supersensible research, the physical incarnation of Christ-Jesus was a unique event in human history, one that cannot be repeated. The true second coming of Christ-Jesus that would begin in the twentieth century (1933) was to be a superphysical process where the Saviour would appear clairvoyantly to select individuals in various parts of the world in an angelic form; that is, occupying his resurrected body. This experience is the same as the blinding event that occurred centuries before to St. Paul on the road to Damascus.

Understandably, Rudolf Steiner had to distance himself and the German Section of the Theosophical Society from such serious esoteric falsehood which could have potentially sabotaged the actual reappearance of Christ-Jesus in the twentieth century. Even prior to the "Coming of the World Teacher" announcement, an irrevocable fault-line had developed between the Western Theosophical school of Rudolf Steiner and the Eastern Theosophical school of Annie Besant. This was indicated by Steiner in the esoteric lesson of 1 June 1907:

> Now, however, the Western school has become independent, and there are two comparable schools: one in the East, the other in the West—two smaller circles instead of one large one. The Eastern school is being led by Mrs. Annie Besant, and those who feel more attracted to her in their hearts can no longer remain in our school ... [T]here must be an esoteric school of the West and an esoteric school of the East ... One of these schools is led by Mrs. Besant, the other by Dr. Steiner. But we have to decide which one to follow. (From a lecture entitled the "Tau and Rose Cross" and published in *The Secret Stream: Christian Rosenkreutz and Rosicrucianism*; 2000)

In 1912, after Rudolf Steiner refused to allow members of the Order of the Star in the East into the German Section,

President Besant revoked the Section's charter. As a result, Steiner and a group of prominent German supporters officially left the Theosophical Society in February 1913, along with 2,500 other members from 55 out of the 69 lodges in the German Section. So began the Anthroposophical Society.

7.2   Anthroposophy Breaks Away from Theosophy

The establishment of the Anthroposophical Society by Rudolf Steiner was a clear Rosicrucian admission that Theosophy—the Movement and the Society—had both failed to achieve their intended great purposes and had fallen beyond any hope of repair. Fortunately for human development, Anthroposophy successfully instituted what Theosophy had failed to do—to openly advance the stream of esoteric Christianity into the intellectual life of modern civilization.

The Anthroposophical Movement (though it had not then acquired that designation), actually began in 1894 with the publication of Rudolf Steiner's first book, *The Philosophy of Spiritual Activity*. In conformity with the Johannine stream of esoteric Christianity, the Anthroposophical Movement was established as a universally-accessible path of esoteric knowledge—*not* a new religion. This path of esoteric knowledge was adapted to the intellectual requirements of the current scientific age and therefore became the first authentic "science of the spirit" in modern life. Since the Anthroposophical Movement was esoterically connected to the impulses of Christ-Jesus in the supernatural realm through association with the Rosicrucian brotherhood, it was also an esoteric movement, not simply a secular or a religious movement.

The General Anthroposophical Society was instituted by

Rudolf Steiner at the Christmas Conference in 1923–24. Though it was founded as a worldwide, legally-registered society in the public domain, it was also an esoteric society due to its association with the Rosicrucian Order and the spiritual impulses of Christ-Jesus that consequently flowed through it. Though the Theosophical Society was the first, worldwide, esoteric public society in world history, the Anthroposophical Society was the first such society with a truly Western Christocentric orientation.

Regarding the Anthroposophical Movement and Society, it's important to understand that even though Rudolf Steiner was a pupil of Master CRC for a time and, as one of the twelve bodhisattvas, is a Rosicrucian teacher as well, anthroposophy is not merely an extension of Rosicrucianism; it is not simply the modern-day form of the original Rosicrucian stream. Anthroposophy is in fact an entirely independent offshoot of the Rosicrucian Order, and which therefore runs parallel to it. The Rosicrucian Order didn't just morph into Anthroposophy, but had to separately continue alongside it as a hidden fraternity. This was because the Rosicrucian Order continues to guard, on mankind's behalf, a wealth of profound esoteric knowledge that civilization is as yet unprepared to responsibly receive. In a true sense, then, Anthroposophy is the public face of the hidden Rosicrucian Order, its doorway to the world through which transformative esoteric wisdom can be safely divulged for human progress.

Moreover, unlike Madam Blavatsky's dire oath of secrecy to the Western occult brotherhoods, Rudolf Steiner, with the trust and blessing of Master CRC, was entirely free to reveal or withhold whatever Rosicrucian teachings he felt humanity was prepared to receive.

As an independent offshoot of Rosicrucianism, anthroposophy is a major branch in the mighty stream of esoteric Christianity that is under the world-direction of St.

John the Beloved. As such, its central mission is also to fathom, to unveil and to divulge the greater mysteries of Christ-Jesus. Esoteric Christianity, in whatever form that it historically takes, does not seek to preserve or perpetuate the ancient pagan mysteries. Wherever possible, however, as an esoteric path to higher knowledge, anthroposophy will seek to uncover the truth of the old Luciferic mysteries and to place them in the context of the new Christian mysteries. But this does not mean that Rudolf Steiner was somehow the founder of "the new Mysteries" or that he established "a new Mystery school." The life of Christ-Jesus is the foundation of the new mysteries, not Rudolf Steiner. Anthroposophy's mission is to research, study, comprehend and communicate these new Christian mysteries. Spiritual science seeks "to find new answers" *not* "to found new Mysteries."

7.3   Spiritual Science not Mystery Religion

As Rudolf Steiner tirelessly repeated, anthroposophy is a "spiritual science," an intellectually-rigorous method of esoteric research whose aim is to discover natural and supernatural truth. It is not a religion: Mystery, Christian or otherwise. When the natural science of anthropology researches and studies the ancient Mysteries, this does not mean that anthropology has thereby established some "new mysteries" or become a "new Mystery school." Likewise, when the spiritual science of anthroposophy researches and studies the ancient mysteries, this does not mean that anthroposophy has thereby established some "new mysteries" or become a "new Mystery school."

It is also important to understand that the Christocentric focus of anthroposophical spiritual science is not the result of sectarian religious belief, but the result of establishing an esoteric fact through supersensible investigation. The objective research of spiritual science has discovered that the incarnation of Christ-Jesus is *the* central, pivotal event in human history around which all other events revolve. This is the spiritual scientific equivalent of Nicolaus Copernicus (1473–1543) discovering that the sun is the central, pivotal centre in the solar system around which all the other planets revolve. The heliocentric focus of natural science is not the result of sectarian scientific bias, but the result of establishing a physical fact through sensory investigation.

Even though Rudolf Steiner had free and unconditional access to Rosicrucian esotericism, any insights he revealed to the world were always filtered through the prism of spiritual scientific scrutiny. This was, of course, strictly necessary in order to establish anthroposophy as a legitimate method of esoteric enquiry, rather than just a purveyor of tradition, personal opinion or unquestioned belief from the past. To emphasize once more, Rudolf Steiner was not just an uncritical mouthpiece of the Rosicrucian Order, but rather an independent Rosicrucian initiate who opened up Rosicrucian wisdom to a troubled world through his own spiritual scientific investigations.

To be absolutely clear, then, as an esoteric Christian avenue to the truth, anthroposophy's mission is not to create new mysteries, but to open up *all* mysteries: ancient and modern, pagan and Christian, Eastern and Western to the bright light of day consciousness and intellectual understanding.

.

CONCLUSION

SINCE MANY prominent and influential anthroposophists today remain entranced with the seductive allure of "anthroposophy as Mystery school/religion" and who continue to somnolently distort the true mission of spiritual science, it make take some time and effort to correct this unfortunate state of affairs. Nevertheless, as an authentic esoteric Christian institution, the General Anthroposophical Society can confidently rely on the rectifying supernatural assistance of Master John (Christian Rosenkreutz), Master Zarathas (Master Jesus), Master Thomas (Rudolf Steiner), St. Michael and of course Christ-Jesus himself.

As for current and future anthroposophical members, the lesson to be learned from this unfortunate (but not entirely unpredictable) situation is to be constantly vigilant. A prior lack of vigilance resulted in the fiery destruction of the House of St. John on New Year's Eve in 1922. Moreover, it is also important to constantly keep in mind that not all occult assaults on anthroposophy are external. In this case the psychic assailment is subtle and internal, which of course makes it all the more difficult to detect and to positively correct.

NOTES

INTRODUCTION

1. Interestingly, St. John has also significantly contributed to exoteric Christianity, since his Gospel writings established the path of Mystic-Christianity that is used in the lesser mysteries of the Church. Likewise, St. Paul promoted both streams of Christianity: exoterically through his missionary work in Rome, and esoterically through his Athenian convert, Dionysius the Areopagite (whose mystical teachings were later recorded in the sixth century by Pseudo-Dionysius, which writings were later used by St. Thomas Aquinas in his works). Concerning Dionysius, Rudolf Steiner has stated:

   > External history does not know that Paul founded the esoteric school in Athens that was under the guidance of Dionysius. In this esoteric school of Christianity, intimate pupils were given the occult knowledge you are now getting to know through the science of the spirit. (*The Christian Mystery*; 1998)

2. Zeylmans van Emmichoven was one such attendee at

the Christmas Conference who wrote in his book, *The Foundation Stone* (2002):

> Already from the first speech, from the way in which Rudolf Steiner spoke and began with a particular sign, it was immediately evident that a deed was being done which led the whole history of the Mysteries of humanity into a new phase.

As well, later anthroposophists who did not attend the Conference, such as Rudolf Grosse, continued to expand and expound on the "Mystery" interpretation of the event in his book, *The Christmas Foundation: Beginning of a New Cosmic Age* (1984), as evidenced from the following phrases:

- the Mystery site of the 20th century, Dornach Hill [the site of the Goetheanum]

- the Goetheanum as a Mystery Centre.

- the Christmas Conference. The spirit guiding it and, acting as a cosmic artist-being, bringing about this new *social* creation, this spirit would be the Spirit of the Goetheanum, the Spirit of the new Mysteries.

- [Rudolf Steiner] brought the stream of the Michael Mystery down to earth.

3. In a lecture given on 21 August 1911, Rudolf Steiner gave a detailed explanation of why Lucifer has a characteristic, deep-seated yearning for the past:

> During the Moon evolution there were powerful Beings, exalted Beings, who however in a certain respect did not reach the goal of their Moon evolution. Among these exalted Beings was a host under its own leader which, when the Moon

evolution came to an end and the evolution of the Earth began, had not attained the goal of its own evolution. Now this host of Beings entered into Earth evolution, and participated in the guidance of humanity, but always with this tragic longing for a cosmic star which had been cast out of the Moon evolution in the way I have described in the book *Occult Science*. Within the spiritual evolution of the Earth are mighty, highly significant Beings, with their leader, who, because they had to quit the Moon and go on to the Earth without having reached their full development, really feel this yearning for a star outside in the cosmos which they regard as their true home, but to which they cannot attain. These hosts are the hosts of Lucifer. Lucifer himself takes part in Earth evolution with the perpetual longing within him for his true home, for the star Venus outside in the cosmos. That is the salient feature of the Luciferic nature seen from the cosmic aspect. Clairvoyant consciousness comes to know just what the star of Venus is by entering into the soul of Lucifer, thus experiencing from the Earth Lucifer's tragic longing, like a wonderful cosmic nostalgia, for the star Phosphorus, Lucifer or Venus. (published in *Wonders of the World*; Rudolf Steiner Press; 1983)

CHAPTER 1

4. This planetary ancestor of the earth was beyond the current scientific calculation of time (that is, prior to the Big Bang). It existed as a large, liquid-etheric sphere that was an elemental combination of the forces and substances of both earth and moon. Much later in planetary evolution, these forces and substances

separated, and the present moon is the condensed, rigidified remnant of this previous planetary condition. Since this earth ancestor was a combination of earth and moon, esoteric science has termed it the "Ancient Moon" phase of the earth. It was also during this primeval planetary condition that our animal-like human ancestors received an independent astral vehicle.

5. A certain mystery still surrounds the being of Lucifer. Since his current celestial sphere of activity extends from sun to Mars, he would appear to be one of the spirits of movement (known also as dynameis or virtues). His association with cosmic wisdom and reputation for having "fallen" from a previous high estate, however, strongly suggests that he properly belongs with the spirits of wisdom. This idea was also repeatedly indicated by Rudolf Steiner in a Helsinki lecture given in 1912, as in the following statement:

> [T]he normal spirits of wisdom have as companions those who have remained behind and who have become light bearers—Light—Lucifer—Phosphoros" (see Lecture 10 in *The Spiritual Beings in the Heavenly Bodies and the Kingdoms of Nature*; 2011)

An additional unanswered question for many esoteric researchers is whether Lucifer's fall from grace was altruistically motivated (to promote human freedom) or for entirely selfish reasons (due to egotistical pride?)

6. Esoteric Christianity does not regard Yahweh-Elohim (or Jehovah) as God Almighty, but rather as the highest initiate of the angelic kingdom. Due to superior advancement, however, he currently functions at the level of a power (or exusiai). Unlike most progressive powers (and planetary spirits), Yahweh-Elohim works from the

periphery of the moon, rather than from the sphere of the sun.

7. More specifically, the astral body together with the egoic self-awareness was separated from the physical body. Since the upper part of the etheric or life body was also driven out, this permitted the pupil to remember the supernatural experience; but it was also the reason for the death-like, cataleptic condition of the physical body.

8. In a lecture given on 27 November 1906 entitled "Esoteric Christianity," Rudolf Steiner stated:

> The truth is, the Christian esotericism is the most profound which has ever been brought to mankind. Christian esotericism was brought to the earth by that very Being Himself with whom one must be united. It is a question of belief in the divinity of Christ.

Moreover, in a lecture given in 22 December 1923, he further stated:

> [W]hoever really understands the Mystery of Golgotha [the foremost Christian Mystery] understands all the previous [ancient] Mysteries. (Published in *Mystery Knowledge and Mystery Centres*; 2013)

CHAPTER 2

9. Basically, "pantheism" is the belief that the entire universe; that is, everything in nature, is an aspect of God and is not a separate creation. "Emanationism" is the belief that everything in nature is an emanation, an effusion from God (analogous to rays of light from the sun) and therefore is directly connected to him.

10. The absence of any knowledge concerning repeated earth lives; that is, reincarnation, within the mainstream Church was by direct instruction from Christ-Jesus himself. This strict admonition is very loosely indicated in scripture when the disciples Peter, James and John questioned Christ-Jesus about Elijah, who had appeared together with Moses in the transfiguration. Christ-Jesus explained to them that John the Baptist was the reincarnated Elijah, but to "Tell the vision to no man, until the Son of man be risen again from the dead" (Matt 17:1–13). This statement is interpreted by Christian esotericists to mean: "Do not publicly teach the truth of reincarnation until the second coming of Christ-Jesus in etheric form, which will begin in the early twentieth century.

CHAPTER 3

11. More specifically, according to Theosophical literature Shambhala was situated on a sacred island in a prehistoric sea now occupied by the Gobi Desert:

> An island, where now the Gobi Desert lies, was inhabited by the last remnant of the race that preceded ours; a handful of Adepts—the "Sons of God," now referred to as Brahman Pitris ... This sea existed until the last great glacial period, when a local cataclysm, which swept the waters south and west, formed the present great desolate desert. ("Theosophy," Vol. 42, No. 3, January, 1954)

12. This is the name given to the Atlantean sun-initiate in Hindu literature:

> And Manu was imbued with great wisdom and devoted to virtue. And he became the progenitor of a

line. And in Manu's race have been born all human beings, who have, therefore, been called Manavas. (the *Mahabharata*)

In the Sumerian *Epic of Gilgamesh*, his name is Utnapishtim. In an earlier Akkadian account, *the Epic of Atra-Hasis*, the Deluge hero is named Atra-Hasis. In Greek mythology, it is Deucalion who repopulates mankind after being saved from the Great Flood. In Genesis, he is of course the well-known figure of Noah.

13. Of this Atlantean connection, Rudolf Steiner has written:

> The Northern [migratory stream from Atlantis], certain parts of which remained behind in Europe, thrust forward into Asia. While new cultures were being prepared there and were running their course, the population of Europe lived through the centuries as though waiting for something. Their forces were being held back for what was to come. The heart of their cultural life was influenced by the great initiate who took upon himself this area that extends into Siberia and who is called the initiate Scythianos. (*Deeper Secrets of Human Evolution in the Light of the Gospel of St. Matthew*, 1985)

Scythianos was, not surprisingly, one of the twelve bodhisattvas sent out from Shambhala. As Steiner has indicated above, one of his leadership responsibilities was within the geographical area known in antiquity as Scythia, a vast area covering present-day Central Asia, Russia and the Ukraine. Scythian-related tribes are also believed to have extended into Scandinavia, Scotland, Ireland and Germany. According to Charles William Heckethorn, the northern Drotte Mysteries were Scythian in origin:

The priests of Scandinavia were named Drottes, and instituted by Sigge, a Scythian prince, who is said afterwards to have assumed the name of Odin. Their number was twelve, who were alike priests and judges. (*Secret Societies of All Ages and Countries*, Volume 1; 1875)

We know from esoteric research that the Scythian prince who took the name of Odin was one of the twelve bodhisattvas—the master who later became Gautama Buddha.

14. "The Ancient and Accepted Rite of the Thirty-Third Degree is the only cohesive Masonic group run on truly international lines. The Supreme Council in London is one of many Supreme Councils in various parts of the globe, of which the senior is the Supreme Council of Charleston, USA, which effectively operates a worldwide network of Freemasons in the most powerful positions in the executive, legislature, judiciary and armed forces as well as industry, commerce and professions of many nations" (Stephen Knight; *The Brotherhood*; 1985).

15. "Deism" is the philosophical position that the universe was created by an undefined first cause (God) that exists separate and apart from the universe that was created. As a result, human beings can have no direct contact with the creator through revelation, prayer or mystical union. Knowledge of the creator, however, can be derived from the reasoned study of the natural world. Deism was popularized in the eighteenth-century by the well-known French thinker, Voltaire (1694–1778).

16. Public exposure of the Masonic secret of Jahbulon has led one Masonic group in England, the Supreme Grand Chapter of Royal Arch Masons, as of February 1989, to

remove the controversial three-part pagan word for God from the ceremonial triangle used in their ritual. This of course does not mean that Jahbulon is no longer used elsewhere by other Masonic groups, or that it is no longer contained in Masonic literature.

17. As stated by Hall:

> The initiated brother [of the higher degrees] realizes that his so called symbols and rituals are merely blinds fabricated by the wise to perpetuate ideas incomprehensible to the average individual. He also realizes that few Masons of today know or appreciate the mystic meaning concealed within these rituals. (*The Lost Keys of Freemasonry*)

The practice of deliberate obfuscation is also echoed by Pike:

> The Blue Degrees [that is, the three lower degrees] are but the outer court or portico of The Temple. Part[s] of the symbols are displayed there to the initiate, but he is intentionally misled by false interpretations. It is not intended that he shall understand them, but it is intended that he shall imagine that he understands them. (*Morals and Dogma*)

18. Masonic apologists attempt to publicly distance themselves from "Illustrious" Albert Pike's Luciferian doctrine of Freemasonry in a number of ways. One is to say that Brother Pike does not dogmatically speak for all Masonry. While that may be true, he is held in such high regard in the "Mother Supreme Council of the World" that his body is the only one buried within the walls of the House of the Temple in Washington, D.C. Moreover, his esoteric opus *Morals and Dogma* remains the most widely known and read book in Freemasonry, and is still

presented to 32° initiates today.

Another common strategy is to allege that the quoted words were never spoken by Pike, but by a contemporary defamer named Leo Taxil (aka Gabriel Jogand). Though Masonic brother Taxil was a thoroughly disreputable character who admitted to elaborately defaming Catholicism and Freemasonry concerning false reports of demon conjuration (known as the "Taxil Hoax"), he wasn't the original reporter of Pike's infamous Luciferian "Instructions." Pike's address was actually recorded by the well-known French esoteric author Abbe Clarin de la Rive in *La Femme et l'Enfant dans la Franc-Maconnerie Universelle*, and was not fabricated by Taxil as part of his defamatory hoax.

CHAPTER 5

19. In the words of Rudolf Steiner:

> The temptation is too great that people would idealize fanatically a [Rosicrucian] person bearing such authority, which is the worst thing that could happen. It would be too near to idolatry. This silence, however, is not only essential in order to avoid the outer temptations of ambition and pride, which could probably be overcome, but above all to avoid occult astral attacks which would be constantly directed at an individuality of that calibre. (Lecture of 27 September 1911 in *Esoteric Christianity and the Mission of Christian Rosenkreutz*, 1984)

20. The fact that Rudolf Steiner is one of the twelve bodhisattvas is clearly indicated in a response he gave to a question about his relationship to Christian Rosenkreutz. Steiner's reply was in the form of a symbolic picture (an

"Imagination") wherein there is an altar in the supersensible world and beside it on the left stands Christian Rosenkreutz in a blue stole and beside it on the right stands Rudolf Steiner in a red stole. It is clear from this image that these two initiates are equal in stature, serving at the altar of Christ in different but complementary ways (blue and red). So if Christian Rosenkreutz is a bodhisattva, then Rudolf Steiner must logically be one as well.

While it is also true that Christian Rosenkreutz was Rudolf Steiner's teacher for a time, it is not unusual for the bodhisattvas to exchange pupil and teacher roles in different incarnations. For example, even though Siddhartha Gautama as a "buddha" is currently at a higher level of attainment than Christian Rosenkreutz, who remains a "bodhisattva," on occasion Christian Rosenkreutz still acts as arch-mentor to Gautama, his illustrious pupil.

Esoterically, Rudolf Steiner is known by various names, the most common being Master RS. It is customary to refer to certain masters by the initials of a recent incarnation; for example, Christian Rosenkreutz is also referred to as Master CRC; Master Kuthumi (Koot Hoomi Lal Singh) is also referred to as Master KH; Master Morya (El Morya Khan) is also referred to as Master M. From his outstanding incarnation as St. Thomas Aquinas, Rudolf Steiner is also lesser-known as blessed Master Thomas.

CHAPTER 6

21. Though they are united in their dedication to Christ, the bodhisattvas ("masters of wisdom and harmony of feelings") each have specific geographical and cultural areas of responsibility. Master John (Christian Rosenkreutz) and

Master Zarathas (Master Jesus) are Western masters who oversee European development. In an esoteric lesson entitled the "Tau and Rose Cross" (1 June 1907), Rudolf Steiner stated the following:

> At the head of our Western school there are two Masters: the Master Jesus [Zarathas] and the Master Christian Rosenkreutz [St. John]. And they lead us along two paths: the [Mystic-]Christian and the Christian-Rosicrucian way. The Great White Lodge leads all spiritual movements, and the Master Jesus and the Master Christian Rosenkreutz belong to this Lodge.

The reason why Master Zarathas is also known as "Master Jesus" is because he was the second Jesus-child that was born in Bethlehem, who died prematurely at the age of twelve and who then indwelt the virginal Jesus-child until the age of thirty.

22. Blavatsky readily acknowledged that the material in *Isis Unveiled* had been telepathically conveyed to her, as partially indicated in the following quotation:

> I maintain that *Isis Unveiled* contains a mass of original and never hitherto divulged information on occult subjects … I defend the ideas and teachings in it, with no fear of being charged with conceit, since neither ideas nor teaching are mine, as I have always declared; and I maintain that both are of the greatest value to mystics and students of Theosophy. (*My Books*; 1891)

23. As described by Rudolf Steiner:

> Take the affair with the sliding doors through which the Mahatma Letters were apparently inserted, when in fact they had been written and pushed in by someone outside. The person who pushed them in

deceived Blavatsky and the world. Then, of course, it was very easy to tell the world that she was a fraud. But do you not understand that Blavatsky herself could have been deceived? For she was prone to extraordinary gullibility. (Lecture of 12 June 1923; *Spiritualism, Madame Blavatsky, and Theosophy*; 2001)

CHAPTER 7

24. "In Theosophical thought, Jesus lived a century and a half earlier than the official version of history suggests. His role was primarily that of providing a body for the temporary incarnation of the Lord Maitreya, the bodhisattva of the current root race. He attained adeptship in a later incarnation as Apollonius of Tyana" (John Michael Greer; *The New Encyclopedia of the Occult*; 2003).

SELECT BIBLIOGRAPHY

(in alphabetical order)

- Charles William Heckethorn, *Secret Societies of All Ages and Countries* (Cosimo, Inc., 2005)

- H.P. Blavatsky, *Isis Unveiled* (The Theosophical Publishing House, 1972)

- H.P. Blavatsky, *The Secret Doctrine* (Cambridge University Press, 2011)

- Manly P. Hall, *The Lost Keys of Freemasonry of the Secret of Hiram Abiff* (Penguin, 1923)

- Manley P. Hall, *The Secret Teachings of All Ages* (Wilder Publications, 2007)

- Rudolf Grosse, *The Christmas Foundation: Beginning of a New Cosmic Age* (Steiner Book Centre, 1984)

- Rudolf Steiner, *Cosmic Christianity and the Impulse of Michael* (Anthroposophical Publishing Co., 1953)

- Rudolf Steiner, *Deeper Secrets of Human History in the Light of the Gospel of St. Matthew* (Rudolf Steiner Press, 1985)

- Rudolf Steiner, *Esoteric Christianity and the Mission of Christian Rosenkreutz* (Rudolf Steiner Press, 2005)

- Rudolf Steiner, *Mystery Knowledge and Mystery Centres* (Rudolf Steiner Press, 2013)

- Rudolf Steiner, *Spiritualism, Madam Blavatsky, and Theosophy* (Anthroposophic Press, 2002)

- Rudolf Steiner, *The Christian Mystery* (SteinerBooks, 1998)

- Rudolf Steiner, *The Knights Templar: The Mystery of the Warrior Monks* (Rudolf Steiner Press, 2011)

- Rudolf Steiner, *The Mission of the Individual Folk Souls in Relation to Teutonic Mythology* (Rudolf Steiner Press, 2005)

- Rudolf Steiner, *The Secret Stream: Christian Rosenkreutz and Rosicrucianism* (Anthroposophic Press, 2000)

- Rudolf Steiner, *The Spiritual Beings in the Heavenly Bodies and the Kingdoms of Nature* (Steiner Books, 2011)

- Rudolf Steiner, *Wonders of the World, Ordeals of the Soul, Revelations of the Spirit* (Rudolf Steiner Press, 1983)

- Stephen Knight, *The Brotherhood : The Secret World of the Freemasons* (Harper Perennial, 2007)

- The Holy Bible, *RSVCE* (Ignatius Press, 2006)

www.ingramcontent.com/pod-product-compliance
Lightning Source LLC
Chambersburg PA
CBHW021934040426
42448CB00008B/1061